A RIVER OF BLOOD

A RIVER OF BLOOD

Two Centuries of Conflict Along the Kennebec River

By Gerard W. Gawalt

© 2023 by Gerard W. Gawalt

All rights reserved. This book or any portion thereof may not be reproduced or used in any manner whatsoever without the express written permission of the publisher except for the use of brief quotations in a book review.

ISBN: 9798342648936

TABLE OF CONTENTS

Dedication · vii
Introduction · ix

Chapter 1   Bad Beginnings · 1
Chapter 2   War Comes To The Kennebec · · · · · · · · · · · · · · 25
Chapter 3   River Runs Red · 59
Chapter 4   The Final Abenaki and English War Along
              the Kennebec · 121
Chapter 5   The Revolutionary Finale · · · · · · · · · · · · · · · 135

Epilogue · 161
Acknowledgements · 165
Bibliography · 167
Index · 173

DEDICATION

To Jane, my wife and best friend, who continues to support my writing efforts. Thank you.

INTRODUCTION

This is a story of dispossession, violence and hope. The interactions of the Europeans and the Abenaki People were conflicted from the start. Both had different aims and both approached issues with very different cultural and psychological outlooks and experiences. Even with the best of intentions conflicts were likely. Their intentions were not always good, and sometimes they were just evil.

In 1600 before the English settlers began to arrive, the Kennebec River teemed with salmon, sturgeon, striped bass and many other fish and shellfish. Fur and fresh bearing animals, like white tailed deer, moose, river otters and beaver provided clothing and sustenance to the Kennebec Tribe.

Like other rivers in Maine, for example the Androscoggin and the Penobscot, it provided a living to the hunter/gatherer tribe of Abenaki who lived on its shores and lived on its bounty.

These rivers were not only important routes to the interior but their fertile river bottom land was ripe for agricultural planting. For these reasons, the rivers were attractive to English settlers looking for new homes, despite the fact that native tribes already used the rivers and the valleys. Conflict was inevitable and it would not be bloodlcss.

Although the Kennebec River valley and its inhabitants are central to this book, it is important to remember that they were a very small part of the centuries-long saga played out in eastern North America by the Europeans and the Indigenous peoples.

During these two centuries the English, Indians and French suffered a nearly continuous series of raids and wars. After each war the number of Natives declined due to deaths or migrations to Canada. After each war the number of English settlers increased. After each war both sides agreed to a treaty. Unfortunately, they spoke to each other, but they did not hear what the other was saying. In retrospect the conclusion was inevitable. At the time, participants saw no end to the struggles.

The Kennebec River was the lifeblood of the Abenaki tribe that lived on it and in its valley. It was the main artery of their travel from the ocean to the deep woods as the tribe followed its annual routine hunting and gathering in tune with the seasons and the plants, fish and animals that provided them sustenance

The Kennebec River became the main route for the Eastern Abenaki (Abnaki, Abanaki, Oubenaki) tribes to connect to the Native tribes in Canada and later their French allies. The Kennebec (Long river) and the Chaudiere rivers were the main waterway to the St. Lawrence River and Quebec. At the same time the Kennebec River through the Sebasticook and Souadabscook Rivers was the main waterway in the interior to the Penobscot River and therefore the main water route from the Penobscot River to Canada.

For these reasons the Abenaki with their French allies fought to maintain control of the Kennebec and the English struggled to gain control of the river. The waters of the Kennebec were the lifeblood of the Wabanaki living along it. Over the century from 1675 to 1775 thirty-five years of open warfare on the Kennebec often turned the river red with blood.

Jesuit missionaries came to the Kennebec late in the seventeenth century and supported the Abenaki's attachment to the French and against the English settlers. They were just a part of the French missionary activity in the Dawnland. Often the situations were complicated by the competition among the Jesuits on the St. Croix and Kennebec, the Recollects on the St. John and the Capuchins on the

Penobscot. In their efforts to attract and hold Indian converts they often led the opposition to the English settlers.

Long before the first European sailed into the Kennebec River, it had been a bloody waterway as local tribesmen battled Indigenous tribes to their north, east and west. Fellow Alkonquians from what is now Canada were no friends of Abenaki residents along the Kennebec River valley. They raided the locals and retreated to their home villages, while the Kennebecs returned the violence. Mohawks found the Kennebec and the Penobscot Rivers easy routes to attack the coastal Abenaki villages. Mi'kmaqs from the north also attacked the coastal and riverine Abenaki tribes in the sixteenth and early seventeenth centuries. Life could be tough for the Abenaki tribes before the English arrived. It would only get tougher.

Even today, historians tend to have a simplistic view of relations between Europeans and Natives. The relations between Europeans and Indigenous People of the various tribes of Natives was very complex depending on inter-tribal and intra-tribal competitions for territory, food, furs and European goods and alliances.

In 1634 William Wood said: "The country as it is in relation to the Indians is divided as it were into Shires, every several division being swayde by a several king." Native groupings were very complex. Even individual tribes had local subdivisions and leaders. All had different names for other tribes. Wars, plagues, migrations and shifting alliances made for a very fluid situation, as Alden Vaughan commented, while trying to describe the various groupings of Natives.

Shifting alliances and conspiracies raced through the Dawnland like the frequent Nor'easters that batter the Maine coast.

Warfare was not carried out on a European scale or style. It was a system of raid and retreat, mainly because the nomadic hunter/gatherer tribes lacked the resources for intensive warfare, according to anthropologists like Wendell S. Hadlock. Mi'kmaqs raided Penobscots ((Bezegowak, Panawahpskek, People of the Rocky Place), Kennebecs (Canabis, Quinibecki, Kennebis, Kinnibki),

Passamaquoddy(Tolakutinaya) and other Abenakis. Mohawks (Haudenosaunee People of the Longhouse) even raided Maine tribes. Wawenocks raided Pennacooks and Massachusetts tribes. Abenakis, including Kennebecs, raided Massachusetts tribes every fall for corn and captives. Historian Alden Vaughan asserts that the Eastern Abenakis devastated the Massachusetts tribe in the early seventeenth century.

So too the southern Pennacooks and western Mohawks fought their traditional enemies along the Kennebec and Androscoggin rivers.

Each tribe was centered around one river valley and they vigorously defended their territory.

Many Natives simply sought personal glory and captives to exploit. Kidnapping, killing, torture, rape and even cannibalism were part of the raid. Captive women and children were most likely to be exploited and enslaved. Men and older boys were most likely to be killed and tortured. As the years passed, the capture of enemies became more and more a financial/business transaction replacing the fur trade as a source of money to purchase European goods. The result was fewer deaths and less torture of English captives at the hands of the Abenaki.

Indians captured by the English during warfare were often abused and enslaved. Women and children were most frequently turned into servants, but they usually simply ran away.

The Natives welcomed European traders who brought clothing, guns, metal utensils and weapons; they built an economy based on the fur trade; they tolerated European fishermen; they feared and hated English settlers.

Europeans welcomed the Native fur procurers; they occupied lands wherever and whenever they wanted; they feared and hated Native warriors; they exploited Native women.

The desire of Natives for European goods changed their economic and semi-nomadic culture. Along the Kennebec River the Abenaki relied on a seasonal variable subsistence economy of hunting, fishing, gathering and planting. Even as the Natives began to plant more corn, they settled into moveable seasonal villages and their economy became commercial. Once the Indians became accustomed to European goods and guns there was no going back to a world without metal products, without guns, without rum, and without other manufactured products, even clothes. Once Natives were dependent on Europeans, it became only a question of which ones. They had to find the means to pay for these products. The fur trade, redemption of captives, the "sale" of land and piracy became sources of income.

At first traditional inter-tribal rivalries prevented a unified response to the European invaders. Natives tried to ally with what they saw as European tribes of French, Dutch and English to gain an advantage over their traditional enemies and obtain the much desired and soon necessary European supplies and weapons. It would not be beneficial to the tribes of the "Dawnland."

As a result the future of the Indigenous people was tied to the European success or failure of their chosen ally. When the Eastern District tribes allied with the French to drive out the English, their future became dependent on the outcome of the centuries long conflict between France and England. It would not be beneficial to the tribes of the Dawnland. It was the story of dispossession and violence.

It was also a story of deceit and misinformation. Throughout the many treaties over the centuries signed by English and Native leaders both sides often deceived their opponents during the negotiations. Both sides misinformed their opposite negotiators as to their intentions and their authority to negotiate treaties that made promises of protection for people, property, land ownership and land usage. Both sides misunderstood what their opponents said or wrote into the treaties. Because the Abenaki had no written language, the treaties were written in English words unknown to the Abenaki. Because the various Abenaki "tribes" spoke variant languages, translators for the English and the Natives could not clearly convey the meanings of words-spoken or written. For example, John Gyles who had been a captive of the Maliseets for nearly nine years was often employed as a translator. But Gyles had his own problems with the English language.

In the minds of the Natives the French held advantages over the English. The French were interested in controlling trade and territory, but there were not many French settlers. The French did not come in family groups, so the men "married" Native women. The French brought Catholic priests who spent their lives living in Native villages and providing counsel and religion. They championed the Natives against the Protestant English. They became part of the fabric of Native life, rather than competitors.

Intra-tribal differences became important as some Indians wanted to accommodate to life with the English settlers and those who wanted to drive the English out of their territories.

As the fur trade declined Abenakis turned to land "sales," piracy and the sale/ransoming of captives to finance their purchase of Europeans guns and supplies. So too, Englishmen turned to the cash sale of scalps to provincial governments and the sale of captured Indians as slaves.

The Massachusetts government issued fifty edicts authorizing the payment for scalps between 1675 and 1760. Official records show that there were 94 separate claims for 375 scalps. It is revealing of the culture of the times that the French, English and Natives engaged in the same process.

There may have been no savages in the Dawnland, but there was plenty of savagery on all sides of the conflicts on the Kennebec.

Geography proved to be very important and very hard to understand. Maine is filled with 5,575 named lakes and 32,000 miles of rivers and streams

The Kennebec-Chaudiere river corridor between the Atlantic Ocean and St. Lawrence River was important to the Natives and later to the French and English as a major artery for trade and war in the Dawnland.

A River of Blood: Two Centuries of Conflict on the Kennebec River

The Kennebec River (Kinapekintak or Kinibecki in English translated Abenaki–meaning large body of water or long river)) is about one hundred and seventy miles that leads from the Atlantic Ocean at Merrymeeting Bay (chisapeak in Abenaki-"at the big part of the river) to the heart of the Dawnland and was the most direct route to the region that became Canada.

The Androscoggin River (Alassikantek in Abenaki/English meaning river of rock shelters or the People where the pollock are plenty) also emptied into the Merrymeeting Bay but came from a more northwestward direction than the Kennebec.

Four other rivers, the Cathance, Eastern, Muddy and Abagadasseta also empty into Merrymeeting Bay, but the Kennebec and Androscoggin are by far the largest rivers. And the Kennebec provides the best and largest access to the ocean and the interior.

The names of the Indigenous Tribes, like virtually everything we know about their lives and cultures, were and are still filtered through the eyes and minds of Europeans. Unfortunately the Natives had no written language, so that even the "dictionaries" for Indigenous peoples were devised by Europeans. And oral traditions and historical accounts became warped and then faded away.

The English tended to name the local Native tribe after a geographic location-hence the Kennebec, Androscoggin, St. John and Penobscot. The Kennebecs were also known as Caniba, Kinibek, Kinibecki, Kennebis or Abenaquis. Englishmen translated the Abenaki words kinibec or kinibecki as "bay" or "long river" which the English used for the entire Kennebec River and the tribe that lived there. The "Androscoggin" tribe was called Ansagunticooks or Ammoscongon by the tribe's members. The Pasamaquoddy called themselves Peskotamuhkat. The Penobscots called themselves Panawapskewi or Pennawahpsek. The Eastern Abenaki or Wabanaki tribal name was usually the tribal word for "The People." For example, Wabanaki means "Easterners" or "The People of the Dawn" as the first people to greet the sun each morning.

Abenaki is said by some to be a derivative of Wabanaki (variously spelled Wapaachis, Wabanakie and Wobanakies). The sacred white stone of the Abenakis was called the Waban Aki , the symbol of purity, protection and spiritual connection. Abenaki has also been spelled in many ways, such as Abenaques or Abenaquois. Further complicating the issue, is that the Indigenous People had no written language so that any European name is usually based on a phonetic spelling of a spoken word or phrase.

As a result, contemporaries and historians have used various names with different spellings. Many of them appear in this book. For this sometimes confusing lack of unity, I apologize.

Noted expert, Robert Guzmet estimated there were less than 12,000 Natives in what is now the state of Maine up to and including the St. John River tribes of Echemins or Maliseets (Malecites, Good River People) and Souriquois or Mi'kmaqs. Estimates of Native numbers for what is now New England vary widely from 60,000 to 200,000. The number of Indigenous People would soon be reduced by epidemics in 1616-1619, 1634, 1648-49, 1689-1690 and 1702. Smallpox, measles, influenza, diphtheria, and a variety of viral and bacterial infections swept through the natives. Because the tribes of the Dawnland were scattered and thinly populated, they escaped the devastation inflicted on the more southerly tribes.

Not just the English were to blame. Membertou, a leader of the Mi'kmaqs, claimed that before the arrival of the French "his people had been as thickly planted as hairs upon his head." But now they were a scattered few.

This historian could find no direct evidence on how the tribe on the Kennebec was affected. Some recent scholars estimate that ninety-percent of some tribes died and the remaining survivors scattered into the hinterlands. Some southern New England Indians found refuge among the Wabanaki, adding additional strains and stress to the local tribes, such as the Kennebecs.

Europeans saw the devastating effects as a " God given" boon. As John Winthrop wrote in 1629: "God hath consumed the Natives with a miraculous plague, whereby the greatest part of the country is left void of inhabitants."

They then used the deaths of the Natives as God's authority to take their land. "For the natives in these parts, God had hath so pursued them, as for 300 miles space, the greatest part of them are swept awaye by the small poxe, which still continues among them: So has God hathe hereby cleared our title to this place," crowed Winthrop to Sir Samuel D'Ewes in a 1634 letter.

Many English colonists would agree with Samuel Penhallow, when in his 1726 history of the Indian wars, described the Natives as "bloody pagans" and "monsters...Who are as implacable in their revenge, as they are terrible in the execution of it, and will convey it down to the third and fourth generation." Penhallow was correct that blood feuds were an intricate part of Indian life and war.

The Kennebec River is widely considered the dividing line between the farming/hunting Indigenous People whose cultivated crops provided most of their sustenance and to the east/north the hunter/gatherers of the Dawnland who depended mostly on wild animals, uncultivated crops, fish and shellfish for their sustenance.

The Kennebec tribe also found itself on the middle ground between the English and the French. Both nations claimed the land of the Kennebec River valley. As a result, chiefs of the Kennebec tribe, such as Rawandagon, enjoyed leverage against both the English and the French. They tried to use it for their own and their tribe's benefit. Their problem was English settlers and traders wanted the region more than the French.

Until the Europeans arrived, the Indigenous People followed a mostly peaceful routine of spending summers near the mouth of the river and winters inland.

This peaceful routine was regularly disrupted by raids from neighboring tribes of Abenakis or the more distant Mohawks (Haudenosunee People), Alqonquins along the St. Lawrence River and Mi'kmaqs and Maliseets from further east along the coast. For example, in 1606 the Mi'kmaqs raided the Abenakis on Mt. Desert

Island and the next year the Abenakis raided the Mi'kmaqs killing Panonias, the son-in-law of the Mi'kmaq leader, Henry Membertou. The next year Membertou led the Mi'kmaqs, now armed with guns and steel hatchets from the French, on a raid on the Pennacook village of Chouacoet at the mouth of the Saco River. Caught by surprise by the seaborne attack, the Abenakis were overwhelmed. The Mi'kmaqs killed or captured most of the Abenakis. Membertou bragged that he "had killed twenty savages and wounded ten or twelve." It is believed by historians that this was the first occasion when one native tribe used European weapons against another tribe in the Dawnland.

A Jesuit, Pierre Biard, told his Superior in 1611 that "the Irocois are known to the French chiefly for the perpetual warfare which they maintain against the Montagnais and Alconquins and friendly tribes."

Moreover, according to Biard, "they are even said to have been addicted to the eating of human fresh, and the Excommunicated and Armouchiquois tribes (includes the Kennebecs) are said to have the same practice even now."

In turn the Kennebecs would raid neighboring tribes or less frequently venture north to attack the "Canadian" tribes. Kennebecs and other Abenakis would annually raid the Pennacooks and the tribes in Massachusetts for corn and captives. Enemies were captured and/or killed. Sometimes the torture and killing of enemies provided entertainment for the Kennebecs. Usually women and younger children were kept as slaves. Sometimes the Kennebec River flowed with blood even before the arrival of Europeans.

The Eastern tribes also found themselves as the objects of missionaries. Mostly French Catholic priests but also Protestant/Anglican ministers tried to convert the Abenaki. Not that Protestants expected much success. As Samuel Sewall wrote to William Ashurst in May 1700: "It will be a vain attempt for us to offer Heaven to them if they take up prejudices against us, as if we did grudge them a living upon their own earth."

A River of Blood: Two Centuries of Conflict on the Kennebec River

The Massachusetts General Court ordered the banishment of all Catholic missionaries in May, 1647 and in 1700 the punishment was increased to life in prison. Then they sanctioned the death of the French priest, Father Râle, with the Kennebec tribe.

Not that settlers in the Maine district were particularly religious. As Charles E. Clark wrote: The people of Maine were "reluctant Puritans." Churches and ministers were few and far between.

Unfortunately, the religious competition also fell along national lines.

The Abenaki had their own religious culture, based on a belief in a Supreme Being, Tabaldak (The Owner), who was the creator of everything. They also believed in a number of deities, such as Nokemis (grandmother) and Gluskabe (the trickster), who had supernatural powers and created the Penobscot River. Animals were also spirits: Rabbit was the symbol of trickery and the raccoon the symbol of mischief. Among the Gods of the Abenaki was Pamola (Thunder) who lived on Mt. Katahdin. The Indians tried to avoid going on the mountain for fear of disturbing Pamola in bringing down wind and cold. More importantly, the competition between the three religions for the souls of the Natives added yet another element of conflict between the Europeans and the Indigenous People.

One editorial note, spelling in the seventeenth and eighteenth century writings has not been modernized in this book. Likewise the dates used in this book are those used at the time of the writing or event and have not normally been marked with dual dates. The old calendar year ended March 25. So, for example, a letter written before 1752, dated January 21, 1721 if modernized would read January 21, 1722.

This is the story of two hundred years of conflict along the Kennebec River. It is not a history of conflict in the entire Eastern District of Massachusetts or the Dawnland to the Abenakis. It was just a small part of the larger European and Native Peoples' conflicts throughout eastern America and Canada during the first two centuries of English colonization. The French and their Native allies fought the English and their Native allies. When the English and their Native allies won, the English fought each other in the American Revolution.

In the end there would be no sharing of power. There would be no amalgamation of English and Indigenous Peoples' cultures. Despite their best efforts the Wabanaki tribes would find the English invasion was unstoppable. There would not be enough Wabanaki left to impact the English settlers' lives. The Dawnland would completely become the Eastern District of Massachusetts.

Through all the violence the mighty Kennebec flowed wild and free.

CHAPTER ONE
BAD BEGINNINGS

Europeans had long fished and traded along the coast of the Dawnland, as the local Wabanaki tribes called the present area of Maine. Sometimes they caught more than fish. Sometimes they caught Natives. Sometimes those Indians caught the fishermen.

The Natives welcomed European traders who brought clothing, guns, metal utensils and weapons; they built their economies based on the trade in furs, English captives/scalps and piracy; they tolerated European fishermen; but they feared and hated European settlers.

Bartholomew Gosnold in 1602 came to the Dawnland near present day Bristol in the ship *Concord*. Gosnold, a barrister from Olney, Suffolk, returned with lumber, sassafras and furs, but no captive Natives.

Three years later, after James I became king of England and Scotland, British captain George Weymouth (Waymouth) arrived at Monhegan on May 17, 1605 in the *Archangel*. Then he traveled to Muscongus Bay (fishing place to the Abenaki) on May 30. That is when the trouble started and the battle lines between the Indians and English were set.

On June 4 Weymouth kidnapped five Abenakis near Pemaquid (some say present day Boothbay) to bring to England. According to James Rosier, a member of the crew tasked with recording their adventures, Weymouth lured three Indians on board the *Archangel* with promises of "bread and english peas." Three of their companions fled but were later seduced with presents. Two were seized and carried aboard the ship, while one escaped into the woods. Rosier argued that Weymouth decided to capture the Natives after becoming convinced the Indians planned to kidnap and or kill him and members of the crew.

Rosier also justified their treatment of the Abenakis in describing them as "a purblind generation, whose understanding it hath pleased God so to darken, as they can neither discern, use, or rightly esteem the valuable riches in the midst whereof they live."

Perhaps Weymouth was simply following orders like those given to Martin Frobisher in 1576 to bring some Natives back to England which he had done. Weymouth was actually carrying on a long tradition of European invaders capturing Indians, because recent genetic findings indicate that Vikings from Iceland captured Indian women and brought them back to Iceland, where they interbred with Icelanders.

Anyway, Weymouth brought five Abenakis back to England where he gave three to Sir Fernando Gorges and two to Sir John Popham.

As we will see, three of the Abenakis, Sassacomoit, Tahenedo, and Skidwarres (Skidowarres) returned to their tribes on subsequent English expeditions.

While the Europeans including the English had been active on the coast of the Dawnland for many years, the first real English effort to establish a colony or plantation came in 1607.

The Popham Colony was established in 1607 by Englishmen under the Plymouth Company in a hostile land labeled the "Land of the Bad People" by the explorer, Giovanni da Verrazano. Often called the first European settlement in Maine, it actually followed a French settlement founded by Samuel de Champlain on St. Croix Island near the present town of Calais.

The English settlement was on the west side of the Kennebec River at Sabino Head across Atkins Bay from the fort near the present day Maine State Park. Led by men naive in the culture of the

Natives and the harsh character of the Dawnland, it was ill-fated from the start.

The area around Popham and present-day Bath/Phippsburg was called Sagadahoc (Sunkerdahunk) meaning "mouth of big river" by the local Abenaki tribe.

There were four Abenaki villages or sub-tribal groups along the Kennebec when Popham arrived:Sagadahocs, Cussenocks, Taconnets and Norridgewocks.

The settlement was named for Sir John Popham of London, who was one of the main financial backers of the Plymouth Company and Lord Chief Justice of England. John Popham's new world interest was piqued when he was given two captured Wabanakis by Fernando Gorges, who had received them from Captain George Weymouth.

With knowledge of the atrocities committed by previous European explorers, probably from Tahenedo, one of the captives, the local tribe, called the Kennebec or Sagadahoc by the English, was not friendly. The company had sent a ship captained by Thomas Hanham and Martin Pring in 1606 to explore the Maine coast with the guidance of Tahanedo, one of the captured Natives. Hanham and Pring returned with glowing reports. Tahanedo did not return, choosing instead to remain with his tribe on the Kennebec.

The following year George Popham, nephew of John Popham, and Raleigh Gilbert led the colonizing effort. Young Popham had as a guide, another captured Wabanaki, Skidwares, who had spent two years in the Gorges household. Fernando Gorges described Popham "as an honest man, but old and an unwieldy body, and timorously fearful to offend or contest with others that will do oppose him; but otherwise a discreet, careful man."

Raleigh Gilbert, on the other hand, was "desirous of supremacy, and rule, a loose life, prompt to sensuality, little zeal in religion, humorous, headstrong and of small judgment and experience, other ways valiant enough."

The venturers left "the Lizard" in Cornwall on June 1, 1607.

Young Popham commanded the ship, *The Gift of God*, while Raleigh Gilbert, captained the *Mary and John*. Gilbert was the son of Sir Humphrey Gilbert and the nephew of Walter Raleigh. They promptly became separated but eventually each found their way to the Kennebec River after stopping at Monhegan Island. When they arrived at the Kennebec both anchored together.

Their guide was one of the captured Abenakis, Skidwares (Skicowaros or Skidowarres).

Skidwares led Gilbert in a small boat to the Pemaquid Peninsula, from where he had been captured. They marched across the peninsula to the nearest Indian village, where they met another former captive, Tahenedo (Nahanada), who reportedly "came upon them and embraced them, and made them much welcome, " according to Fernando Gorges in his *Brief Narration*.

This self-deception by the English proved to be dangerous. Skidwares quickly left the English for his own tribe, promising to return as guide, but "he heald not his promysse."

Not impressed by the narrow Pemaquid River, Popham and Gilbert sailed westward to the Sagadahoc River, now known as the Kennebec. On August 17 two captains in their ships' boats sailed up the river looking for a suitable site for their colony. Finding no other place more suitable for a fort and village, they returned to the mouth of the river. "All went ashore and there made choice of a place for our plantation which is at the very mouth or entry of the river Sagadahock on the west wide of the river, being almost an island of great bigness," according to the manuscript, A Briefe Relation of the Discovery and Plantation of New England.

Local historian Parker Reed says they landed at Hunniewell's Point and then occupied Horse-catch Point. The precise spot is still in doubt.

This was the arrival of the first group of English settlers in the Dawnland. The Natives quickly resented the arrival of these groups of settlers, particularly when the settlers were happy to appropriate the small areas cleared in the dense forests by the Abenaki.

After a brief religious service, the planters set to work on August 20. Not only did they construct houses and a stockade fort, but they also began construction of a sloop, soon named *Virginia*.

The stockade was made of earthen berms topped with a wall of wood and was to enclose barracks, officers' quarters, houses, store rooms, barns, a chapel and a truck house. The placement and control of truck houses or trading posts with the Natives would become a central point of contention and control of the relations between the Europeans and the Native tribes. The plan called for twenty buildings, four bastions, and mounted cannons. It is not known how much of this plan was constructed.

Popham was the president of the Company and Gilbert the military commander.

While the one hundred and twenty settlers built shelters and Fort George, the Indians began "to beat a trade with him for furs." The English could not survive long without food supplies from the Natives, who wanted to trade for English goods but did not want a permanent European settlement in their midst. In fact their hostility convinced the English to remain close to the fort.

No blood was shed, but life was on the edge.

Tahenedo(Nahanada) and Skidwares arrived with nine canoes of men, women, and children on September 5. After a cordial but brief visit, the Indians returned to Pemaquid with a promise to guide the English to the "bashabe" or principal chief. Four days later Gilbert led a trading party to Pemaquid but they found no Indians "no living creature. They were all gone from thence." Gilbert and crew had to return to the Kennebec.

Soon some of the local Natives arrived including one who described himself as Sebanoa, "Lord of the River of Sagadahock." Shortly Gilbert went upstream where he met with Sebanoa, but neither man trusted the other.

In early October, Sebanoa, Naheneda and Skidwarres all arrived at Fort George in canoes. The English entertained them and they all attended a religious service led by Reverend Robert Seymour.

Shortly after, on October 8, the *Mary and John* returned to England. Unfortunately, the ship had no cargo of furs. Fernando Gorges reported to his associates that there was "confusion" and "childish factions" among the colonists as to their jobs. But he assured them there are "rich furs if they can keep the Frenchmen from the trade," fish, masts for ships, and even grapes for wine "much like the wine that comes out of France."

The *Gift of God* left the Kennebec in December arriving in Plymouth in early February bearing even more bad news about the colony. Gorges reported that the weather was severe, the soil was barren, there were growing factions among the colonists, and the colonists were "disgracing the other, even to savages." Gorges wanted King James I to help with a ship, supplies and money.

The Natives were falling under the influence of the French according to Gorges. "The French are in hand with the natives to practice upon us, promising them, if they will put us out of the country and not trade with none of ours, they will come unto them."

After the departure of the two ships, only about forty-five Englishmen remained, according to a later report by John Smith.

Then George Popham, who according to Gorges "had long been an infirm man" died on February 8, 1608, promoting Gilbert to the leadership post.

A Jesuit, Pierre Biard, believed that the Amouchiquois (Kennebecs) had killed him by magic.

And then Gilbert returned to England, leaving the colonists virtually leadership. They quickly began mistreating and cheating the Indians. Fear quickly led to panic.

Two ships with supplies arrived in December, temporarily bolstering the English plantation.

Then the fort and several dwellings burned. Exactly when is not known. The 45 remaining colonists soon suffered from the cold and a shortage of food. The Abenakis did not offer to feed them, in part because they had moved upriver in the annual movement to secure their own food.

According to a letter of Jesuit Pierre Biard, a Jesuit missionary in Canada who later visited the abandoned site in 1611, in their second year "the English, under another Captain, changed their tactics. They drove the Savages away without ceremony; they beat, maltreated and misused them outrageously and without restraint; consequently these poor abused people anxious about the present and dreading still great evils in the future ."

According to Biard, the Indians decided to "kill the whelp ere its teeth and claws became stronger."

Meanwhile, Gilbert was notified by a boat in the summer that his brother, John Gilbert, had died making him heir to a large estate. He returned to England on the same boat. The remaining colonists finished work on their own ship, the pinnace, *Virginian*. They were ready to leave if necessary. That opportunity soon arrived.

English blood soon flowed on the Kennebec. Biard reported to his Provincial Superior: "The Opportunity came one day when three boat-loads of them went off to the fisheries. My conspirators followed in their boat, and approaching with a great show of friendliness (for they always make the greatest show of affection when they are the most treacherous) they go among them, and at a given signal each one seizes his man and stabs him to death. Thus were eleven Englishmen dispatched." This report from a French missionary sympathetic to the Indians, whom he was trying to convert.

Thus convincing the remaining survivors to flee back to England by September of 1608. They arrived in late November. The grand Popham colonizing experiment was over. The United States government later built forts Popham and Baldwin on the site of Fort George.

The Wabanaki still remained in sole possession of the Kennebec River valley. But not for long.

English vessels, some sent by Sir Francis Popham, continued to fish and trade along the coast of the Dawnland and unfortunately continued to capture Indians as trophies and slaves. Biard reported in a January 22, 1622, letter to his Superior in France, that he had gone from Port Royal to "Kinibeque" with M. Jean de Biancourt in October 1611. They were worried because two English ships at "Emmetenic" (Matinicus Island) had captured two Frenchmen. They found the location of Popham, which he declared beautiful and convenient. When they ventured up the river they were surrounded by "six Armouchiquois canoes" with twenty-four warriors. "They reconnoitred, they carefully noted our numbers, our cannon, our arms, everything." The Indians then lured them into an ambush by promising they could get corn from the "great sagamore Meteourmite" who was "an enemy of the English and whom they supposed to be an enemy of all foreigners." It turned out, he only hated the English.

But they escaped the warriors' ambush and traveled upriver where they met Meteourmite "in the royal apparel of a savage majesty." Biard says he was greeted with "a thousand demonstrations of friendship." He prayed with them and "gave them some crosses and pictures." He then blessed the children. On a subsequent visit Biard said he followed the same routine.

Father Biard said Meteourmite was friendly toward them and prevented the warriors from killing them, even returning some hatchets and bowls that the Natives had taken from their ship. Biard reported that he was pleased with their visit and their meetings with the Penobscots on their return trip to Port Royal.

After their first disastrous attempt to establish a colony on the Kennebec, the Pophams sent two ships in 1608 to the midcoast area. Once again Sir Francis Popham, son of John, landed in the area of Pemaquid, where the native Wawenocks (Round Island) were not as strong as the tribe on the Kennebec and where fishermen were a common sight. Pemaquid (long point" to the Wawenocks) was a peninsula approximately nineteen miles long and eight miles across at its widest point.

Six years later Captain John Smith was exploring the Maine coast and while anchored at "Monhiggin" reported that he saw "a ship of Sir Francis Popham" sitting "right against us in the main" and that "hauving used for many years onely that Porte, the most" of the fur trade "was had by him."

Small fishing villages sprang up along the coast, between the Kennebec and the Pemaquid River, putting more pressure on Abenaki/English relations.

The Indians also tried to use the English against their own traditional enemies. John Smith reported in 1614 that Dohoday of Sagadahoc extracted a promise from him to help against the Tarrantines at Penobscot in return for trade and friendly relationships with the Wabanaki.

After the failure of the Popham settlement, fishermen and individual traders continued as early and regular visitors to the Kennebec River region. Natives were eager to trade for European steel, iron, guns, powder, beads (wampum) and even cloth. Europeans were eager for furs.

Unfortunately we do not know what the Natives thought about the English appearances. We don't know if the Natives believed the reports of Skidwares and Tahenedo about what they had seen in London. Were they honored for their knowledge or ostracized for lying and exaggerating about the numbers and power of the English nation. They would soon learn for themselves.

We do know that the Abenaki on the Penobscot and Kennebec rivers fell increasingly under French influence—witness the appearance of the Jesuit Father Biard, on the Kennebec shortly after the failure of the Popham Colony.

Father Biard, who had visited the Kennebec tribe, tried to establish a French colony on Mt. Desert Island in 1613. Biard and Enemond Masse led a group of French settlers from Port Royal and established a village called Saint Sauveur. Within a year an English ship commissioned by Sir Thomas Dale, governor of Virginia, and commanded by Samuel Argall while on a fishing expedition attacked and destroyed the French colony.

Argall had been told by local Indians of the French settlement on Mt. Desert. According to a report in *Jesuit Relations*, the French were totally unprepared for the Englishmen's sudden attack. The French, including a religious brother, fought back, but after several deaths the French surrendered.

Father Biard reported that they "expected only death or at least slavery." Most of the French returned to French posts further Eastward, but Father Biard was brought to Virginia by Captain Argall. Dale sent Argall north again to finish the destruction of French outposts, bringing Father Biard with him.

He finished the destruction of Saint Sauveur and went onto the St.Croix River, where he forced the French to flee. Capturing a local Native, Argall convinced him to lead them to the French at Port Royal, but there was no one there. On November 9, 1613, Argall turned southwestward to return to Virginia.

Father Biard and other French captives were brought to England in early 1614 and allowed to find their way to France.

In 1625 Edward Winslow went to the Kennebec in a shallop loaded with corn and brought back 700 pounds of beaver and other skins. Governor Bradford gave this account of the Plymouth Colony's first trading venture to the Kennebec River. "After harvest this year, they sent out a boat's load of corne forty or fifty leagues to the eastward, at a river called Kennebeck; it being on one of those two shallops which their carpenter had built them the year before, but bigger vessel had they none. They had laid a deck over her midships, to keep the corne dry, but the men were faine to stand it out in all weathers without shelter, and that time of year begins to grow tempestuous; but God preserved them and gave them good success, for they brought home 700 pounds of beaver, besides some other furs, having little or nothing else but this corne which themselves had raised out of the earth. This viage was made by Mr. Winslow and some of the old standards for seamen they had none."

Encouraged, traders, known as The Undertakers, from the Plymouth Company established a trading post on the Kennebec in 1628 at Cushnoc (also Cushenoc, Kouissinox, Coussinox Abenaki for "where the tides run no higher"). A spot the English labeled "the convenientest place for trade." This site is now near old Fort Western in Augusta. A location far up the river and far into the Kennebec tribal lands.

They also sent one of their members, Isaac Atherton, to London in 1626 to secure a royal patent on lands on the Kennebec.

From the Crown via the Council for New England they received control of fifteen miles on each side of the Kennebec up to the Nequamke (Nequamkike) Falls, about five miles below the Taconic (Tecconet, Ticonic) Falls . They were granted not only ownership of the land but control over all commercial, maritime and settler access. They were also authorized "to take, apprehend, seize and make prize of all such persons, their ships and goods as shall attempt to inhabit trade with the savage people of that country."

This patent covered territory between what is now Gardiner and Waterville. Cushnoc became their anchor.

About the same time the English established a year-round village at Pemaquid, which became the northernmost English outpost confronting the French and Indians in the Dawnland. Later, General John Winslow would build Fort Western on the Cushnoc site (much later Hallowell then Augusta). The Plymouth Company also had local truck houses at Popham and later Richmond.

John Howland was in charge of the trading post. Natives brought furs to Cushnoc for guns, steel knives and hatchets, as well as "coats, shirts, ruggs, shirts, biskett, pease, prunes etc." . Before long the Indians were abandoning their traditional life cycles of hunting, fishing and foraging to concentrate on commercial trapping and hunting fur bearing mammals, particularly beaver, otter, white-tailed deer and moose. Soon, Kennebec tribal people, encouraged by Jesuit missionaries, began to concentrate further up the river in permanent villages, such as Norridgewock, with log houses and stockades. It was a lifestyle change that could not be sustained by the traditional hunter/gatherer cycles.

It was, as we shall see, an existential change for the people of the Dawnland.

Fishermen/traders continued to ply the coast and rivers leading Governor William Bradford to complain in 1627 of "base fellows" who "begin fishing and fall wholly to trading." He pointed out the "wrongs they did both last year and this, and besides they still continue to truck pieces [guns], powder and shot with them."

Located on the Kennebec River reaching far into the interior, the Plymouth traders soon put some of their rivals to the south out of business. John Winter was located on Richmond Island south of Cape Elizabeth in Casco Bay without any interior connection. On June 18, 1634, he complained to Robert Trelawny: "Heare hath not bin to this Island one Indian all this years, nor to the maine to our house, that brought Any skins to trade. I sent out a boote twyse this last Winter and got not on[e] ounce of bever from the Indians."

It is not surprising that few Indians went to Richmond Island to trade, because of its violent recent history. In 1631 Natives led by Sagamores Skitteygusset and Squidrayset had killed Walter Bagnall and John Peverley and burned their trading house, because they felt cheated in their trades for guns, rum and supplies. The killers were never punished, but two years later Englishmen returned to the island, and hanged an Indian, Manatahqua, a visiting Indian from Massachusetts.. Shortly after Winter wrote his letter, the Abenakis returned to the island and killed two hundred hogs and goats.

Also in the year of 1628 Thomas Purchase, who originally left England in 1626, arrived in the Kennebec area via Saco and began trading.

Four years later Purchase and George Way received a patent from the Council for New England for the land between the lower Androscoggin and Kennebec Rivers. We will see later that this became the basis of the Pejepscot claims to nearly one half a million acres between the Kennebec and Androscoggin rivers..

Purchase settled between the Kennebec and Androscoggin rivers on what became known as Merrymeeting Bay (Nassouac; allegedly named for the Native and English celebrations that occurred there). The Androscoggin (Anasagunticook) Indians accused him of cheating them with watered down liquor, overpriced goods and low prices for their furs. Eventually after a series of skirmishes between the rivers, the Natives burned Purchase's truck house and escaped with the Englishmen's corn harvest. But all that was in the future.

In 1630 Edward Ashley was joined in Penobscot by the Plymouth Company to trade for furs, but he was accused of "trading powder & shote with the Indians" and committing "uncleannes with Indean women." Plymouth leaders dismissed him and shipped him back to England. The next year the French and their Native allies attacked the Plymouth trading house, stole the furs and supplies.

Back on the Kennebec, Bradford reported that in 1633 the Plymouth Company sent "thirty-three hundred and sixty six pounds weight and much of it coat beaver, which yielded twenty shillings per pound, and some of it above" which allowed them to pay all of their debts in England.

Trade began to decline at Cushnoc, but Governor Bradford refused to abandon it and leased it to a private company for one-sixth of the profits. Later in 1651 another English group from Plymouth leased it for 50 English pounds a year, but it was later reduced to 35 pounds. Failure brought a sale of the Kennebec Patent in 1661 to John Winslow for 400 English pounds..

Shortly after, Rawanadon's band of Kennebecs planned to rob the trading post, because "there being store in the Plimouth trading house," but decided it was too well guarded and moved on to break into English houses.

When in 1634 an outsider, John Hocking, tried to invade the Plymouth Company's territory on the Kennebec, he was shot dead, according to William Bradford. Clearly, the English/Indian conflict was not the only source of blood on the Kennebec.

The trading was so lucrative it attracted unauthorized competition. Hocking, an agent of Lords Say and Brooke, the Pilgrims' rivals for the Maine fur trade, was living southward at Piscataqua when he and a small crew sailed eastward to the Kennebec.

Hocking intended to sail up river beyond Cushnoc and to cut off the trade to the Plymouth truck house. When challenged by John Howland, the Cushnoc trader, Hocking replied he "would goe up and trade ther despite of them and lye ther as long as he pleased."

According to Bradford, then "one of the saddest things" occurred on the Kennebec. The Plymouth Company was authorized "to take, apprehend, seize and make prize of all such persons, their ships and goods, as shall attempt to inhabit or trade with the savage people of that country within the precincts and limits of his and their several plantations."

When Howland ordered Hocking to leave, he refused and sailed past the trading post and anchored up the river. Hocking hurled "ill words" at Howland.

Howland then sent two men including Moses Talbot to cut the anchor cable of Hocking's vessel. They succeeded in this action without gunfire, but as the vessel was carried downstream by the current, Hocking took a gun and killed Moses Talbot, one of the Plymouth men.

According to Bradford, Howland could not restrain himself and shot Hocking. The crew fled down the river and returning to Piscataqua reported the incident in their own fashion.

Massachusetts officials then arrested John Alden, who had been at the Plymouth truck house, but according to Bradford had not shot Hocking.

At a conference of Massachusetts and Plymouth authorities, they concluded "they all wished these things had never been, yet they could not but lay the blame and guilt on Hocking's own head."

Both sides were then exhorted to adhere to the spirit of the law and "promising to follow the same," wrote Bradford. Thus ending "one of the saddest things" at the Plymouth land in Maine, according to Bradford.

A year later, Winslow sent 3,738 pounds of beaver pelts to England, and between 1631 and 1635 the Plymouth Company trading post at Cushnoc sent 12,530 pounds of beaver pelts to England. This enabled the Plymouth Company to pay off its debts in England.

Criticizing English traders at Boston, Pemaquid and Penobscot who were selling supplies, guns and ammunition to the French and Indigenous People, Bradford accused them of being "the cheefest supporters of these French."

John Winthrop of the neighboring Massachusetts colony feared the Pilgrims' bad behavior would "bring all and the gospel under a common reproach of cutting one another's throats for beaver."

The Kennebec tribal leaders just sat back and said nothing. They wanted to trade, not fight.

By 1630 it has been estimated that around fifteen hundred Europeans had permanently settled between the Kennebec and Pemaquid rivers. They may have even outnumbered the Abenaki people in that part of the Dawnland.

The several British families on the Kennebec, estimated to be about fifty families by James Sullivan, then settled into a period of relative peace.

Although a French Jesuit had visited the Natives on the Kennebec as early as 1608, the French did little to reinforce their claims to the Eastern Lands as far west as the Kennebec until the 1630's.

After King Charles granted France control of all the area called Acadia in the Treaty of St. Germain in 1632, the French under Claude and Charles LaTour began to assert control over the Dawnland. The Company of New France wasted little time in reinforcing its presence with soldiers, colonists, traders and priests.

The Plymouth Company had built a trading post on the Penobscot. In the fall of 1633, LaTour attacked Thomas Willett's trading post at what is now Castine, killing two men, capturing three others and their goods. "This was the end of that project," according to Bradford.

LaTour and his partner Charles Etienne D' Aulnay set about "to clear the coast unto Pemaquid and Kennebec of all persons whatever," according to Bradford. They set up headquarters at La Heve (later Castine) and threatened to seize any British traders or settlers east of Kennebec.

The French attack on the Plymouth truck house on the Penobscot caused the English settlers at Pemaquid and Kennebec to prepare for the worst. As far west as Richmond Island in the Casco Bay, Edward Trelawny warned on January 10, 1636, that "We must better fortify or else expose ourselves to the loss of all, which may be prevented by a speedy preparation against all assaults."

The growth of the fishing station at Pemaquid into a village with its own trading house and stockade took the pressure off Kennebec as the most eastern English settlement in the Dawnland.

The Council for New England in 1630 had given John Beauchamp of London and Thomas Leverett of Boston a patent to all the land between Pemaquid Point and the Penobscot River. The Muscongus Patent later became the property of Samuel Waldo.

The next year the Plymouth Company of London and King James I granted 12,000 acres and the obligation to transport settlers to Pemaquid to Gyles Elbridge and Robert Aldsworth, Bristol merchants. Abraham Shurte, a long time resident of Pemaquid, had already established a trading post and built a stockade fort in 1630. He became the agent for the Bristol merchants, hence the later name of Bristol for the town encompassing Pemaquid. Shurte, who served as magistrate for thirty years, considered himself a friend of the local Wawenock tribe, who summered on the Damariscotta and Pemaquid rivers. Because of this relative peace, settlers began to prefer the Pemaquid region over the Kennebec, where relations with the Natives remained uneasy.

Pemaquid continued to grow and began exporting oats, hay, oxen and cows. Fish still remained the chief export from Pemaquid,

Sheepscot and Monhegan, while furs became the dominant export from the Kennebec.

Estimates put the English population between the Pemaquid and St. Georges rivers at eighty-four families. Sylvanus Davis estimated there were sixty-eight fishermen in the Kennebec or Sagadahoc ("mouth of the river" to the Abenaki).

In the same year of 1631 Natives led by Skittygusset and Squidrayset killed Walter Bagnall and John Peverley and burned their trading house on Richmond Island in Casco Bay just west of the Kennebec.

Traders at Kennebec and Pemaquid were accused by Governor Bradford of having "filled the Indians with guinness (guns) and munitions to the great danger of the English."

"So in truth the English traders themselves have been the chief supporters" of these French and Indians. Because "the Plantation at Pemaquid (which lies near unto them) doth not only supply them with what they want, but gives them continual intelligence of all things that pass among the English, especially among some of them. So it is no marvel though they still grow and encroach more and more upon the English, and fill the Indians with guns and munitions. To the great danger of the English, who lie open and unfortified, living upon husbandry, and the other closed up in their forts, well fortified, and live upon trade in good security."

Bradford correctly predicted the future: "If these things be not looked to and remedy provided in time, it may easily be conjectured what they may come to." Death and destruction from the Pemaquid through the Kennebec to the Saco river valleys.

The availability of Europeans goods and guns upset the balance between the tribes and they soon began competing for access to trade items and the furs to pay for them. Then their traditional cycle of life was upset by concentrating on commercial hunting fur bearing animals for skins to trade. Later when they had decimated the wild animals they had ended their ability to maintain a hunter/

gatherer culture. The competition between the French and English and occasionally the Dutch exacerbated the intertribal conflicts and often even brought on intra tribal divisions over whether to ally with the Europeans or fight them. Native leaders began to be judged on whether they could provide guns, rum and other European goods.

Massachusetts had been granted authority to arrest, try and punish anyone who sold "munitions" and "gunns" to "arm the Indians against us," and send them to England, but they had little or no control in the Maine frontier.

One of the most devastating smallpox epidemics ravaged New England and the Indigenous tribes in 1634. Although we have no records of its impact on the Kennebec, colonists believed its uneven impact proved that God was on their side. In a 1634 letter to Simond D'Ewes, John Winthrop thanked God for the slaughter of the innocents. "For the natives in these parts, God hath so pursued them, as for 300 miles space, the greatest parte of them are swept away by the small poxe, which still continues among them: So has God hathe hereby cleared our title to this place."

To paraphrase a famous comedian, Jimmy Kimmel, the English were too arrogant to know they were ignorant of the Indigenous people.

That same year the New Englanders began a three year campaign against the Pequot tribe in southern New England. The Pequots were destroyed and the reverberations were felt in the Dawnland including the Kennebec. There the tribes were put on high alert that the English could turn on them. As a result the Indigenous People looked more and more to the French for military and commercial support.

In the aftermath of yet another epidemic and with the decline in the fur trade, Native leaders turned to the French and their Jesuits for help.

The influence of the Jesuit priests, such as Father Gabriel Dreuillettes (Druillet), moved south from Canada and Acadia along the Kennebec and Penobscot rivers. Traveling to the Kennebec in

1646 Father Dreuillettes was known for spending months hunting with the Abenakis along the Kennebec and performing "miracle" cures. Father Dreuillettes became a friend of John Winslow of Cushnoc. Usually he stayed on the Kennebec with the Norridgewock (Nanrantsouac or Moloujoak) . The village was located between two falls on the Kennebec, now known as Madison and Skowhegan. Their tribal leader Oumamanradock asked Father Dreuilettes to travel to Cushnoc and plead with the English traders to stop selling alcohol to his tribe.

No hope there!

The next year the Massachusetts Bay General Court banned Jesuits from its territory. Just another legal shot in the ongoing religious war between Catholics and Protestants in the Dawnland. Father Dreuillettes made his last trip down the Kennebec in 1651-52. In 1980 a replica chapel was built on Riverside Drive in Augusta, where the original chapel was believed to have stood.

The Plymouth Company having cleared its debts and the fur trade on the Kennebec beginning to slide in 1638 sold the trading rights to a private group "being loath it should be lost by discontinuance." The Plymouth government was to be paid one sixth of the profits.

For the next twenty years the Plymouth province maintained civil control of its Kennebec Patent.

Leaping far ahead, the Plymouth General Court bailed out of its Kennebec Patent in 1660, selling to a group of buyers: Antipas Bois, Edward Tyng, Thomas Brattle and John Winslow. For the next century they did little but trade, but their ancestors would profit immensely.

In 1639 Thomas Purchase negotiated a deal with the Massachusetts government, giving him a four mile square section of land between the Androsgoggin and Kennebec rivers and gaining the "due protection of the governor and company" of Massachusetts Bay colony.

Purchase was the object of the Kennebec and Androscoggin tribes ire in 1642. Tribal members raided Purchase s house in Pejepscot. Angered by shoddy goods and low prices for their furs, they accused him of cheating them and took £145 in goods, but did not personally harm him this time.

Thomas Gorges warned his father, Sir Fernando, in 1642 that "the country is in great fear of the Indians. They have all convinced themselves together from the Penobscot to the [Saco] to cut off the English."

Violence and bloodshed came to the Kennebec that year from a more traditional source. Mohawks attacked an Abenaki hunting party on the upper Kennebec, torturing and killing six men and enslaving women and children. Later in 1651, Father Dreuillettes, the first regularly settled religious leader on the Kennebec, warned John Winthrop of the Massachusetts government that the Mohawks intended a general massacre of the Abenakis at Norridgewock (known as Kennebec in New France). In 1662, more than two hundred Mohawks raided the trading post on the Penobscot. And even near the end of the century John Gyles, a captive of the Maliseets, reported that their greatest fear was of the Mohawks.

For much of this period settlers on the Kennebec were without a formal civil government. The Plymouth Company, then the Massachusetts government and then the agents of Sir Fernando Gorges tried to establish authority over the traders, fishermen and settlers without much luck.

In many ways the Dawnland was wild and open to deception, fraud and criminal activity on all sides.

Abenakis, like the sagamore Rawandagon (sarcastically nicknamed Robinhood by the English) eagerly sold land to Englishmen in Casco Bay and along the Kennebec and Sheepscot rivers. Most of which he had no control over and no authority to sell.

Rawandagon, the son of Sagamore Manawormet, had two sons, both came to hate the English. Rawandagon's nickname may have meant Lord of Misrule or simply that the English thought he, like all Natives, were funny characters to be jobbed and robbed of their furs and land. In English parlance, to obtain land cheaply by trickery was called a Robinhood bargain, according to the Oxford English dictionary. As Harold E. Prins speculated, the "English duped" them into signing documents that served as proof that the Indians no longer owned parts of their own country. The English, according to Prins, thought the Natives were "credulous fools" and ripe to be scammed or Robinhooded.

Their tribe, the Kennebecs, lived in the areas known as Kennebec/Merrymeeting Bay/ Sagadahoc Bay/Sheepscot, but they and Rawandagon had influence between Pemaquid and Saco. English guns, liquor and goods had infiltrated Abenaki culture and overwhelmed their lifestyle. They needed something to trade or sell to the English. When furs became scarce or inadequate, local clan chiefs, like Rawandago, turned to selling land. Whether they understood the English concept of land ownership (and I think they quickly did) is not definitively known. But they soon learned what the English thought and they did not all like it.

Often these sales over a twenty-five year period were for alcohol. For example, Rawandagon's land sale for "two gallons of wine and a bottle of strong waters to him in hand paid." Or the 1657 sale of land to an English fisherman for the "yearly pay unto sd Scittergusset, Sagamore, during his life one Trading Coat for Capussicke and one Gallone of Lyquor for Ammocingan."

At the mouth of the Kennebec River, "Chief Robinhood" in 1649 sold Arrowsic Island to John Richards. Arrowsic (Arrowseag in Abenaki, meaning "place of obstruction) is bordered by the Kennebec and Sasanoa(Back) rivers. Richards sold his land to two Boston merchants, Thomas Lake and Thomas Clarke, who established a trading post and stockade there in 1658-1659.

In 1650 "Robin Hood" also sold land which later became Parker's Island, Indian Point or Georgetown in the Kennebec to John Parker.

In 1654 the Plymouth General Court sent Thomas Prince to the Kennebec River to establish a civil government. Meeting at the house of Thomas Ashley sixteen men, appointed John Ashley a constable and Thomas Purchase "assistant to the government." Among the laws accepted were fines for theft and drunkenness. Any inhabitant selling liquor to Indians was fined double the value of the liquor and a "stranger" selling liquor was to be fined £10. Regular courts were to be held at the Ashley house.

All was relatively peaceful there until the overwash from King Philip's War. But the trade was declining, leading a Plymouth Company leader on July 7, 1659, to state that there were "troubles among the Indians" on the Kennebec. "Some having been killed or carried away" discouraged them from hunting and the traders could expect "serious losses" from a "cessation of trade." The company lowered its lease from £35 to £10 and ultimately sold its patent for £400 in 1661 to Artepas Bois, Edward Tyng, Thomas Brattle and John Winslow.

Rawandagon and four other sagamores (Terrumgquin, Weasomanascoe, Scawquet and Abunhamen) also sold land to Reverend Robert Gutch (Gouch) along the Kennebec on May 29, 1660. Neither the exact amount of land or the sum paid are specified but detailed boundaries are in the deed. The 1667 inventory at his death listed six acres. The city of Bath now sits in the midst of the land originally purchased by the Reverend Gutch, who had emigrated from Wincato, England. Gutch had made a brief stop in Salem in 1641 before going to the Dawnland. Gutch preached at several points along Merrymeeting Bay. Gutch and his wife, Lydia, were the parents of seven children. Gutch later drowned, while trying to cross the Back River on horseback on a preaching mission in 1667.

Another example of the Natives selling land, was one thousand acres on Merrymeeting Bay to Christopher Lawson by "Kennebis and Abbagadasset." Lawson came from Boston in 1667 and also purchased land on Swan Island in the Kennebec near the present town of Dresden.

In June 1675 on the cusp of widespread violence between the English and Natives, Rawandagon was still selling land. Again he sold additional land to Thomas Purchase on Merrymeeting Bay near the mouth of the Androscoggin River. Virtually all the land in the lower Kennebec River valley was covered by one Indian deed or another.

In 1670 there were thirty families in what was then called Sagadahoc on the east side of the Kennebec and twenty on the west side, not counting a few at Woolwich. Early historians, such as William Williamson, reported that the entire Eastern district had about one thousand Englishmen of military age in the 1670's.

The Duke of York's agents arrived in 1665 and swore Englishmen to loyalty to the Crown and reported there was no government. They also reported that there were not more than thirty houses in the largest of three settlements east of the Kennebec. "On the North Side of the Kennebec River, which is the bounds of the Province of Mayne upon Shipscot River, and upon Pemaquid 8 or 10 miles Assunder are 3 small plantations belonging to his Royal Highness the biggest of which hath not above 30 houses in it, and those very meane ones too, and spread over 8 miles of ground at least. The People for the most part are fishermen. They have had hitherto noe government and are made up of such as to avoid paying debts and being punished have fled hither; for the most part they are fishermen, and share in their women as they do their boats." The commissioners led by George Cartwright added in their report to Lord Arlington, Secretary of State:: "they are inhabited by the worst of men." Ouch!

Meanwhile for the Kennebec tribe the killing continued. Mohawks raided the Kennebecs and they in turn joined an Abenaki campaign against the Mohawks along the Connecticut River in 1663 to protect their turf and their fur trade.

The Mohawks were the most feared enemy among the Eastern Indians as far north as the Penobscot and St. John River. In 1669 they decisively defeated the Abenakis, chasing them all the way to the Penobscot. Some such as the Reverend Megapolensis accused them of "inhuman homicides" and cannibalism: "the common people eat the arms, buttocks and trunk, but the chiefs eat the head and heart."

Father Dreuilletes had this to say about the Mohawks in a letter to his Superior in Paris: "All the Nations of Savages which are in New England hate the [Mohawks] and fear...lest he will exterminate them. Indeed, he has broken the heads of many of their men, finding them hunting Beaver, without making satisfaction."

Over the next few years, Abenaki "Indians at Kennebeke" led by Rawandagon, raided English farms in the Connecticut River Valley. Blood flowed in both directions along the Kennebec.

Then the Mohawks soundly defeated the Abenakis creating fear and anger among the Native tribes as far east as the Penobscot. Frustrated by their defeats by the Mohawks and the continued incursions of English settlers in their hereditary lands along the Kennebec and eastward to the Penobscot, the Eastern tribes increasingly turned to the French for support and protection.

CHAPTER TWO

WAR COMES TO THE KENNEBEC

English settlers eagerly moved into the region around the Kennebec River and Merrymeeting Bay even though there was no formal civil government. Or maybe it was because there was no civil government.

Among those families were the brothers, Thomas and James Gyles, from Devonshire, England. They arrived in Boston in 1668, just after the great plague of 1666 had decimated the Indigenous people. The next year James purchased land on Merrymeeting Bay and then purchased land on the Kennebec from the Natives and settled on sixty acres along Muddy River. Thomas also purchased land along the Muddy River, the Androscoggin River and 500 acres at Cathance Point. They joined Samuel York, Thomas Purchase and Thomas Stevens.

According to the later memoir of Thomas's son, John, they had been "at a place call'd Merry-meeting Bay, where he had dwelt for several years 'till the Death of My Grand Parents, He with his Family return'd to settle his affairs." In 1676 Gyles returned to the Kennebec area, but he found very few families there and continued on to Pemaquid, where he was killed in an Abenaki attack in 1689 and his wife, two daughters and two sons were captured. Two of his sons, Thomas and Samuel, escaped. One son, James, was tortured and killed at Pentagoet. John was enslaved for nine years. Thomas's wife Margaret and his two daughters were brought to Canada and later ransomed.

After nine years of enslavement young John would gain his freedom; serve as a government interpreter and return to Merrymeeting Bay and the Kennebec region as the commander of Ft. George on the Androscoggin River.

The Kennebec settlements were included in a new county created by the Massachusetts government in 1674. The western areas of York, Kittery and Falmouth had been sending representatives to the Massachusetts General Court since 1669, but there were none from the Kennebec region. All settlements from Kennebec eastward were included in the new county of Devon or Devonshire. Commissioners were appointed to advance "the wayes of godliness" and provide means of marrying, punishing crimes and creating a militia. The militia was organized into five "train bands', with one at Sagadahoc and others at Pemaquid, Damariscove, Cape Newagen and Monhegan.

Thomas Clarke, Humphrey Davy, Richard Collicot and Thomas Gardiner went to "Pemaquid, Cape nawaggen (now Southport) and Kennebec" in July of 1674 and established a new government. Then King Philip's War cut short the Massachusetts efforts to exert "magisterial power in marrying such as are duly and legally published according to the law, as also to punish criminall offences."

While Massachusetts extended its control over the Eastern District, it tried to impose its laws on the Indigenous people within its borders. Indians were subject to the same laws as Europeans, plus a few additional ones. Disruptive or dependent (poor) whites could be banished or "warned out." This could not be applied to Indians, so they were often sentenced to servitude or slavery for a period of time. Particularly disruptive or criminal Indians were sold as slaves to the West Indies.

Puritans passed severe penalties against miscegenation. Unlike the French colonies to the North and East, the English practiced little formal intermarriage or inter cohabitation. However, some historians, such as Alden Vaughan claimed the practice was common in eastern villages and fishing sites where European men greatly outnumbered available White women. Needless to say, most of these laws could not be enforced in the Dawnland.

As hostilities broke out between the Natives and English in New England, the Massachusetts government tried in 1675 to impose a ban on the sale of guns and ammunition to the Wabanakis at Kennebec and Pemaquid. But some English settlers complained.

On the Kennebec the small English garrison at Arrowsic went upriver to Taconic (Takonet) to convince the warriors to turn in their guns and other weapons. The Kennebecs refused, asserting "in case they would not come down and deliver their Arms, the English would kill them."

But even the settlers complained that the Indians needed guns and ammunition. Thomas Gardner of Pemaquid could have been speaking on behalf of all the English traders, when he told Governor John Leverett that "these Indians amongst us live most by Hunting" asking "how we Can Take away their Armes whose Livelihood depends on it." The traders knew that if the Natives could not hunt, they would not have any furs or hides to trade–therefore no profits for the traders. In his September 22, 1675, letter Gardner claimed "these Indians in these parts did never Appear dissatisfied until their Armes were Taken away."

Wabanaki sagamore Moxus also protested to the government.

It would be an ongoing conundrum. Either provide weapons that may be used to kill you, or not provide weapons and provoke the Natives into wanting to kill you.

On July 19, 1675, according to William Hubbard, Rawandagon "with great applause of the rest, made a dance" of peace. So the Abenaki retreated upriver and the English hunkered down near the mouth of the Kennebec. The peace would not last.

The King Philip's or Metacom or Great Narragansetts War began in June of that year, but minor and major hostilities and anger had roiled English/Native relations for decades.

The war began in earnest after English colonists hung three Wampanoags on June 8 for killing a Christian Indian, John Sassamon. In retaliation the Wampanoags attacked the settlers in the area of Swansea killing, wounding and capturing many English settlers.

Then in September hundreds of Nipmucs massacred a wagon train of colonists headed toward western Massachusetts.

In December Plymouth Governor Josiah Winslow attacked the major settlement of Nipmucs and Wampanoags in a swamp near present day Kingston, Rhode Island, killing more than three hundred men, women and children–some were burned at the stake.

Angered and frightened, neighboring Narragansetts then joined the battle attacking settlers at Providence, killing and torturing more than sixty English settlers and twenty Christian Wampanoags.

The troops of the New England Confederation caught King Philip at Mt. Hope in Rhode Island on August 20, 1676. Philip was beheaded and drawn and quartered. The power of the Native tribes of southern New England was nearly destroyed. But this was not the case in the Eastern Lands, where the French and Natives still held the upper hand.

Many members of the defeated tribes fled to New York and the Dawnland where they added to the cauldron of unrest.

It may have been called King Philip's War in southern New England, but in the Dawnland it became known as the First Abenaki War. For two years Kennebecs, their neighboring Anasagunticooks and other Abenakis attacked settlements at Arrowsic, Woolwich, Cape Neddick, Sheepscot, Scarborough, Casco, Falmouth, Pemaquid and many isolated homesteads. Reportedly 260 English settlers were killed or captured and an unknown number of Abenakis were killed and captured.

Death and terror were on all sides of the Kennebec.

Troubles were exacerbated in the summer of 1675, when English fishermen overturned a canoe carrying the wife and child of Squando, sagamore of the Saco Tribe. The child drowned, and according to William Hubbard, a clergyman and Harvard graduate, who wrote his *Narrative of the Troubles with the Indians in New-England* in 1677, "Squando Father of the Child hath been so provoked thereat that he hath ever since set himself to do all the Mischief he can to the English in those parts."

The Kennebecs and Anasagunticooks carried on talks with the English trying to maintain their "Amity." But English traders on the Kennebec and at Pemaquid refused to supply guns and powder to the Natives. The Indians then complained that they were starving without the means to hunt. Hearing of trouble at Casco the Kennebecs moved up the river to their fort at "Totonnock" (Taconic, present day Winslow where the Sebasticook River joins the Kennebec). Captain Sylvanus Davis then sent messengers to the Natives to come down to the trading house to get their supplies, but the Indians misunderstood that there was a threat to them. In the meantime, according to Hubbard, other Englishmen were offering a five pound bounty for a captive Indian.

John Early, a leader at Pemaquid, organized a meeting at Pemaquid with several sachems. There the Indians made many complaints "of the hard dealing of the English in Kennibeck River," but agreed "to keep true Friendship with the English."

West of the Kennebec in Casco Bay, Abenakis attacked in June. Thaddeus Clark provided this account to his mother, Elizabeth Harvey in Boston: "On Friday last in the morning your own Son with two Sons in Law Anthony & Thomas Brackett & their whole families were killed & taken by the Indians, we know not how, 'tis certainly known by us that Thomas is slain & his wife and children carried away captive, and of Anthony & his familie we have no tidings & therefore think they may be captivated."

Clark summarized the situation for his mother: "There are of men slain 11, of women and children 23 killed & taken, and we that are alive are forced upon McAndrew's his island to secure our own. We are so few in number that we are not able to bury the dead, till more strength come to us."

Willaim Hubbard added more details about the rampage by the Kennebecs and other Abenakis: "the said Brackett, his wife and a Negro were all bound by the Indians. His wife had a brother (Nathaniel Milton) who offering to resist was killed forthwith, the rest with five Children were led away Prisoners."

Hubbard continued: "the Indians passing from Anthony Bracketts to Corbins, killed (Robert) Corbin himself with Humphrey Durham, and Benjamin Atwell aforementioned: then passing on to other houses, carried away some of them Captive, and killed others. At one of the next houses, the Woman and children got into the water by a canoo; but one James Rose, his wife and children were carried away; Corbin's wife with one other Men's wives; and the children of another of them, they likewise carried away."

Hubbard reported thirty-four killed and captured.

The English and Natives at Kennebec continued to talk, with the Kennebecs complaining that the English destroyed their corn and then refused to trade for guns and powder. But then, according to Hubbard, "News came to Kennibeck, that the Indians had killed divers English in Casco."

Captain Davis, fearing the worst, then set out sentinels.

Richard Hammond's garrison house at Stinson's Point near the Kennebec in present day Woolwich was attacked on August 12-13, 1676 by the Wabanaki. Fourteen English settlers were killed.

Hubbard provides a detailed account. "Several Indians repaired in the Evening to the House of one Mr. Hammond, an ancient Inhabitant and Trader with the Indians up Kennibeck River. His Daughter or a Maid that was Servant in the House, either naturally afraid of the Natives, or else upon something she observed in their Countenances, or Carriage manifested so much fear as made her run out of the House to hide herself in some Place abroad. The Indians perceiving it, the more to dissemble their Treachery, ran after her, and brought her into the House, telling her (although they could not perswade Her, she grew more afraid than before being now more strongly perswaded that they came on purpose to kill or surprize those in the Family; whereupon she suddenly made an Escape out of the House and presently passed into a Field of Indian Corn, whereby she might the better avoid the Danger of any Pursuer, and so ran across over the Land that Night ten or twelve Miles, to give them Notice that lied at Shipscot [Sheepscot] River; it is said after she got out, she heard Noyse in the House, as if they were Fighting or Scuffling within Doors; but she did not count it Wisdom to go back to see what the Matter was, knowing enough before of their Villaneys, how well so ever her Mrs. (that was more versed in the Trade of the Indians) might think of them. Those of Shipscot taking this warning escaped away as soon as they could, leaving their Cattel and their Dwellings as a Prey to the Indians.

What befel Master Hammond and his Family is not yet certainly known; Reports past up and down, that some who came down the River afterwards, saw some of the Dead stripped upon the Bank of the River, which makes us fear the worst, concerning all the Rest; for certainly the whole Family, sixteen in number, were all at that time either killed, or carryed away Captive, none save the Maid aforesaid being known to make any other Escape, to inform their Friends, like 'Jobs Messengers' what befel the Rest of the Family."

James Sullivan one hundred years later wrote in his *History of Maine*, that Hammond "who built the Business of his trading carried him up to Teconnet Falls, where he was imprudent enough to rob the Indians of their Furs while they were intoxicated."

Whatever the cause of the Kennebecs' anger, after they killed the Hammonds they moved southwestward to Arrowsic Island near the mouth of the Kennebec River.

Abenaki Indians attacked Thomas Lake's house among others at Arrowsic on August 14, 1676, killing, scalping and enslaving more than thirty English colonists. Lake and Sylvanus Davis escaped by canoe to nearby Parker's Island (now Georgetown).

Reportedly, a Kennebec woman was admitted to the garrison house/stockade on the evening of August 13, but during the night she secretly opened the gate and the warriors swarmed in and overwhelmed the English settlers.

Again, Hubbard provides a nearly contemporaneous description of the events from the English point of view. "The Indians having in this manner surprised Mr. Hammonds House, they passed down the River the same Night, but going by another House meddled not with the People, only turned their Canooes a drift, that they might not finde Means afterwards to escape themselves, or help others to do so: possibly their chief Aim being at Arowsick House, they would not Fear of being discovered, make any Attempt upon any Place nearby; wherefore August the fourteenth very early break of day passed over on to the Island called Arowsick, several of them undiscovered lay hidden under the aforesaid House behind a great Rock near adjoyning till the Sentinel was gone off from his Place (who went off it seems sooner than was Reason, considering the Danger), when presently some Indians followed him in at the Fort Gate (as some Report) while others of them immediately seized the Port Holes thereof, and shot down all they saw passing up and down within the walls, and so in a little Time became Masters of the Fort, and all that was within it."

Hubbard continued: "Captain Lake (joynt Owner with Major Clarke of the whole Island) hearing the Bussle that was below, betwixt the Indians and those that belonged to the Place, was strangely surprized, yet himself with Captain Sylvanus Davis and two more, understanding that the Indians had seized the Fort, and killed divers of the English, apprehending it bootless, or rather heartless to stay, as not being able to stand upon their Guard, or make any Resistance, made a shift to find some Passage out at a Back Door, whereby they escaped to the Water-side, where they found a Canoo, into which they all entered and made away toward another Island nearby; this was not done so secretly but the Indians discerned them before they were gone farr; four of them therefore hasted after those that had escaped, in another Canoo, and coming within shot, discharged their Guns upon them, whereby Sylvanus Davis was sorely wounded;

yet making haste, as generally they use to do that fly for their lives, timor addidit alas, they got a Shore before the Indians overtook them. It is said they were strangely dispirited, or else they might easily have defended themselves against their pursuers: But when once Mens Hearts are sunk with Fear and Discouragement, upon a sudden Surprizal, it is hard to buoy them up, to make any competent Resistance: Capt. Davis being sadly wounded, could neither trust to his Legs to fly, nor yet make use of his Hands to fight, yet was strangely preserved; Providence directing him to go into the Cleft of a Rock hard by the Place, where he first landed. The Indians by the glittering of the Sun Beams in their Eyes as they came a Shore, did not discern him; so as lying hid under the Covert of the Hand of Providence, for two Days, he at last crawled a little about the Water Side, till he found a Canoo, whereby he escaped away with his life, much ado be. The other two Men were better foot Men, and parting from Captain Lake made their escape ten or a dozen miles, to the further End of the Island, and so escaped from the Indians, till they found Means to get off. Poor Captain Lake, that a few hours before, slept quietly in his Mansion House, surrounded with a strong Fortification, defended with many Soldiers, is now forced to fly away with none to attend him. "

Davis lived many years, later dying in Boston. Lake's brother, John, continued to believe his brother was a captive petitioning the Massachusetts government on September 15, 1676, to preserve the life of an Indian condemned to death to exchange him for his brother. But the Indian Sam was hung ten days later "at the Towns End."

Hubbard continued: "And as the Awful Hand of Divine Providence ordered things, was as some say, pursued by such Indians as were meer strangers to the Place, that knew not the Masters from the Man, by one of whom he was shot down, as is supposed, soon after his coming ashore. Lieut. Davis heard two Guns by which was thought, and soon after was known so to be, by an Indian which since hath confessed to Captain Davis, that he shot him that Day. Arowsick was taken, which he intended not to have done, but that he held up his Pistol against him, whereas if he had but asked Quarter he should have had his life. Captain Lake was slain at that time although many Hopes were for some Time maintained, that he was taken alive and kept with other Captives, amongst the Indians; and 'tis said the Indians of those parts did not intend to kill him, if they could have helped it: But it was known, that his Hat was seen upon an Indians Head not long after, which made his Friends conclude what had befallen the Owner, that good Man, who might emphatically be so termed in Distinction from them that may truly be called Just Men, and no more: For it seems according to the Just Agreement betwixt himself and his Part-owner of Arowsick Island, it was not his turn this Year to have been upon the Place, but such was his goodness, that he yielded to the Desire of his Friend and Partner, as in his Room and Stead himself to take upon himself that Service in this Time of Danger; it is hoped his goodness in future time will not be forgotten by such as were anyway concerned therein or had Advantage thereby."

Hubbard then provided one of the most detailed descriptions of the settlement at Arrowsic Island. "This Island (called Arowsick from an Indian so named, that formerly possessed it, and of whom it was purchased by one Mr. [John] Richards who sold it to Captain Lake and Major Clark) lyes up ten miles within the Mouth of Kennibeck River; it is some Miles in length, and containeth many thousand Acres of very good Land; where Meadow and arable-Ground are in good Proportion well suited together; within the Fort aforesaid were convenient Buildings for several Offices, as well for Wares and trading, as Habituation: six or several Edifices are said to have been erected. The Warehouse at that time was well furnished with all Sorts of Goods; besides a Mill and other Accommodations, and Dwellings within a Mile of the Fort and Mansion House; some of whose Inhabitants hardly made their Escape upon the first surprizal of the Fort.

All which considered, the Loss that befel the Proprietours at the suprizal of this Island seems to be very great, valued at many thousands; but those that were the owners with others of late Times, have found in their own Experience what Solomon said of old, There is a time to get, and a Time to loose, a Time to keep, and a Time to cast away; a Time to break down, as well as a Time to build. The Persons killed and taken at Kennibeck, both at Mr. Hammonds and at Arrowsick said to be fifty-three".

The Natives scattered with the captured people, goods and scalps back to their villages and camps. Little was heard of the Kennebec captives until January 5, 1676 (new style 1677) when Francis Card (Carder) a captive settler from Kennebec, escaped from the Abenaki and found his way to Black Point on Casco Bay. Card reported that the prisoners "were well, and not much misused, only put to do servile work."

Card, who lived up the Kennebec told the story of his capture on August 14, 1676. "The Indians came to Richard Hammond, Samuel Smith, Joshua Grant, there parting their Company eleven men came up the Kennibeck River to my house, and there took me and my family. Therefore the Rest of their company went to Arowwick, and there took the Garrison: About a Fortnight after came down Kennibeck River, and so went down to Damaris Cove, and there burnt Houses, and killed cattle." Card went on to say that the Natives' number varied between fourteen and one hundred in their attacks on the Kennebec River, Pemaquid, and Casco Bay settlements.

Card reported they first carried him up the Kennebec to their "fort" at "Taconet". But "the Men coming down they brought me and two Men more down for fear of our killing their Women and Children; for they kept their Women and Children at Taconet all the Summer." Then they go further upstream or to Canada for the winter.

Card told the English that the sachems Squando and Mugg planned to destroy the English settlements, even those at Boston.

Card stated that the Abenaki at Kennebec and Damariscotta took captives to Canada and gave "gifts both of Captives and of Goods to the Eastern Indians, to have them go out with them." Madockawando, leader of the Penobscots, merely "doth pretend love to the English."

The surviving settlers on the Kennebec, Sheepscot and Damariscotta rivers fled to the outer islands of Monhegan and Damariscove, according to Hubbard.

And the blood had just begun to flow on the Kennebec.

The Native warriors then returned eastward to attack settlers on the Sheepscot and on to Pemaquid where they destroyed the fort and dwellings.

In September Richard Waldron tricked hundreds of Abenakis and refugees from King Philip's War in Massachusetts. On September 7 Waldron invited several hundred Natives to a "mock battle." After the Natives had fired their guns, Waldron and the local militia seized as many as they could. Eight leaders, including Monoco, Muttawmp, Matoonas and Tantamous, were sent to Boston, where they were tried for insurrection and hanged. According to William Hubbard, Waldron and the militia "seperated the Vile and Wicked from the rest, and sent them down to the Governour at Boston, where eight or nine of the Ring-leaders, such as One-eyed John, Sagamore Sam of Nashaway, chief Actors of the late Outrages and bloody Mischiefs, had Justice done to them soon after." The rest of the captives were sold into slavery in Barbados. As we shall see, Waldron was later killed by Abenakis in 1689.

In retaliation the Wabanakis then raided Wells and York, killing 43 colonists.

Several residents of Merrymeeting Bay, including James Gyles, Ichabod Wisecall and Richard Collecot, petitioned the Massachusetts General Court in September, 1676 "on behalf of the distressed inhabitants of Devonshire for protection from marauding Indians." Receiving little protection in the Kennebec region, James and Thomas Gyles later relocated eastward to Pemaquid.

Partially in reaction to this plea for help, Waldron and the New Hampshire government gave a license to Captain Henry Lawton (Laughton) of Piscataqua to sail down east and capture and enslave any hostile Natives. Lawton hired the *Endeavor* captained by John Horton. They traveled to Machias in November 1676 under pretense of trade, where they seized nine Penobscots who came to trade at Machias. They then sailed to Cape Sable where they seized seventeen Mi'kmaqs. Hubbard wrote that they "did most perfidiously and wickedly entice some of the Indians about Cape Sable who never had been in the least manner guilty of any Injury done to the English, aboard their vessel, or else some other way, and then carried them away to sell them for Slaves." Lawton then sold them as slaves in the Azores to Portuguese slave traders. When the *Endeavor* returned to Boston, Lawton and Horton were briefly imprisoned for "illegal" activity, but were quickly released.

Abenaki leaders pointed to such "perfidious & unjust dealing of som English" as the "Cause of the Indians Rising" through several generations.

In the winter of 1677 Majors Waldron and Frost led an expedition against the Kennebecs. Ninety soldiers and sixty Christian Natick Indians were sent to "subdue the Indians" on the Kennebec and "deliver the English captives in their hands." The force first skirmished with Natives near present day Kittery but learned from the Natives that the captives were "far away."

They then moved on to Penobscot to retrieve prisoners. The Penobscots insisted "that the Captives were given them by Kennibeck Indians, and they must have something for keeping them all Winter, and therefore were not willing to let them go without Ransome," according to Hubbard. The Penobscots demanded twelve "skins" per person. The "skins" were paid in supplies and liquor. William Chadburn, John Whinnick (Winnock of Scarborough) and John Worwood were freed. Before all the supplies could be delivered, fighting broke out between the untrusting sides. Several Natives were killed and four Penobscots, including Madockawando's sister, were captured and brought away in Waldron's ship.

In the spring of 1677 nine soldiers were at Arrowsic attempting to bury the dead from the previous year's attack, when, according to Hubbard's later account,"they were suddenly surprised by a number of Indians that intercepted them before they could recover their Boat, and so all were cut off but three or four that hardly escaped by some other Way than they came."

The Massachusetts government then withdrew its remaining garrison from the Kennebec. The Kennebecs then turned westward killing three at Wells on April 6, two more on April 12, and seven more at York. Two women were captured at Piscataqua on April 14. Further attacks continued around Portsmouth and Black Point on Casco.

The Mi'kmaqs on July 8, 1677, attacked six fishing boats at Port La Tour in Acadia. The Natives initially seized some of the boats including twenty-eight fishermen. Some of the fishermen, including Joseph Bovey, Richard Downs and Robert Roules were put on board a ketch to chase down another ship. But the fishermen overpowered their captors on the ketch, killing two and bringing two to their home ports at Marblehead and Salem, Massachusetts where residents tortured and stoned them to death. Roules later testified that townspeople including women in Marblehead "flocked about them," overpowered the guards, and "got the Indians into their own Hands, and with Stones and Billets, and what not else made an end to them." Savagery was not confined to either side.

By 1678 both sides were ready for peace. The Abenakis represented by Chief Madockawando and representatives of the New York government, which controlled Maine at this point, met near Casco Bay. The resulting First Treaty of Casco closed the First Abenaki War. The Natives recognized the right of English settlements only west of the Saco River, but the English insisted on the right to return to all their settlements at the Kennebec, Merrymeeting Bay and Pemaquid.The English agreed to pay "the grand chief" Madockawando, sachem of the Penobscots, one peck of corn each year for every English settler. In the Natives mind, this meant the English recognized their sovereignty of the land. All captives were to be surrendered without a ransom. The English government would regulate the fur trade at Kennebec and Pemaquid, and the English would be allowed to build a trading post and stockade (Fort Charles) at Pemaquid.

Both sides signed a treaty, but neither side understood the other. As Thomas Hutchinson succinctly wrote: "it is not certain that they understood that they had promised any subjection at all." The Natives did not understand what the English meant and the English did not understand what the tribal leaders were telling them. As a result, this treaty, like all subsequent treaties, was doomed to failure.

They spoke, but they did not hear.

The English failed to pay their pecks of corn. Not only did the English families reclaim their settlements, but more and more English settlers moved on to the areas at Kennebec and eastward. As the English pushed beyond the agreed upon boundaries, the Indians, encouraged by the French, pushed back. It was a formula for disaster that was repeated many times over the next century.

In the aftermath of the First Abenaki War and King Philip's War the tribes of the Dawnland formed a loose alliance, called the Wabanaki Confederation. The alliance was named after the Waban Aki (White Earth) a powerful symbol of protection and spiritual connection in the Abenaki religious beliefs.The tribes of present day Maine, New Hampshire and Acadia shifted in and out of the alliance.

The Mi kmaq, Maliseet, Passamaquoddy (Pestomahkati) and Penobscot were the principal tribes. The Kennebec tribes (including the Norridgewock) and its French counterpart, the St. François (St. Francis, Odanak) Tribe near the head of the Kennebec River, Wawenocks, Pennacooks, and Saco (Sokoki) were smaller tribes allied with the confederation.

The Abenaki were called Adirondacks or "bark eaters" by the Iroquois, who called themselves "meat eaters." The Iroquois and

Abenaki were traditional enemies, but occasionally joined together to fight the English.

Like the Iroquois Confederation, the Wabanaki Confederation held annual meetings at one of the tribes' main villages to discuss the encroachment of the English, their own alliance with the French, and ways to destroy the English enclaves or at least prevent their encroachments on tribal territories, while still maintaining trade with the English.

The Wabanaki Confederation was not formally dissolved until 1862.

In 1679 returning Arrowsic families successfully petitioned Massachusetts Governor Edmund Andros to resettle Arrowsic. Many prospective settlers arrived in the Arrowsic and Kennebec area, but Indian hostility persuaded many like Thomas Gyles to relocate to more settled regions like Pemaquid. As we shall see, Arrowsic and Pemaquid were both looted, burned and mostly destroyed by the Abenakis and French in 1689.

For ten years all groups tried to expand their power and influence. Most of the action was in the New York and Great Lakes region. But the French governor of Acadia, Sieur de Meneval, expanded forts in Acadia, planned a new fort at Pentagoet (the French derivative of the Abenaki word Pentagwet for "where the waters meet; now Castine) and began to station a war ship on the Eastern coast.

Every year that passed the English settlements grew and moved upstream. As the number of settlers increased so did the number of people engaged in the fur trade. Massachusetts tried to regulate and control trade with the tribes of the Dawnland, but by 1670 they had virtually opened the trade to anyone who would apply for a license (and many did not bother) and pay a five percent tax on all furs (and many did not bother).

Every year that passed the Natives became more dependent on English and French trade goods and guns. Every year that passed the number of fur bearing animals declined as commercial hunting expanded. Pressured by growing English settlements and the quest for more and more furs, the Natives were forced further and further up the rivers. It was a process that had no good end for the Abenaki.

Leaders of the Kennebec realized the problem but they had no answer except to turn to the French who could supply the necessary guns and goods without the encroaching settlement.

Seeing the buildup of French forces, the Governor of the Dominion of New England, Edmund Andros, attacked the home/trading post of French Baron Jean Vincent d'Abbadie de Saint Castin on the Penobscot in March 1688. This was an opening salvo of what became known as the nine-year War of the League of Augsburg or King William's War in America.

Like all wars the name meant little to those people fighting and dying on the killing grounds.

In Europe it was France against the Grand Alliance–England, Holland, Spain, Holy Roman Empire and other minor states. In America it was France and her Native allies against England and her Native allies.

Castin's father-in-law, the Penobscot Sachem Madockawando, sought revenge in an attack on North Yarmouth in the fall of 1688. Local Abenakis, no doubt Including Kennebecs, joined Maliseets, Penobscots and Mi'kmaqs. The Barrett family was killed on Cape Porpoise (Arundel, now Kennebunkport) on October 11 and then the Abenaki moved on to ravage Saco in January 1689.

Late in 1688, Massachusetts authorities ordered military men in the Dawnland to seize any Natives suspected of violence towards the settlers. Using this broad authority the commander of Fort Casco quickly grabbed twenty Wabanaki men, women and children as "security risks" and sent them to Boston.

In return Abenaki warriors captured eleven English settlers and burned farms along the Kennebec.

Abenakis led by Kancamagus (Fearless hunter of animals), chief of the Anasagunticooks, attacked Quochech/Cochecko (Dover) on June 27, 1689. Kennebecs were most likely there when twenty–three settlers were killed and twenty-nine were captured and brought to Indian villages as far north as the Penobscot and St. John rivers.

But the French and Natives had their eyes on a bigger prize–Fort Charles and the settlements in the Pemaquid region. The English settlement and fort at Pemaquid had been a shield standing between the Kennebec settlements and the French and Indian allies to the East. That all changed on August 2, 1689 when more than four hundred Abenakis and Mi'kmaqs led by Norridgewock Chief Moxus, Father Louis Pierre Thury and Jean Vincent d'Abbadie de Saint Castin stormed into Pemaquid. For three days the Natives and Frenchmen were killing, burning, looting and capturing English settlers. The fort also surrendered after seven soldiers were killed and nine wounded. So thorough was the destruction that the number of casualties and captives is still not known.

Father Thury reported that they had confessed their sins before leaving Pentagoet, prayed together before the attack, and then thanked God for their victory. Thury also asserted that they did not torture any English people, "but killed immediately, those whom they wished to kill."

One captive, Grace Higiman (Hegeman), later reported that fifty captives were brought to "the Fort at Penobscot." After three years she was brought to Quebec and sold for forty crowns to a Frenchman. She was later brought to Port Royal where she was ransomed and returned to Boston by Abraham Benoit. She testified that while she was there Abenakis from Kennebec and Penobscot, Bomazeen (Bomaseen, Bombazee) Moxus and Madockawando's son, brought scalps and captives to Quebec for which they received twenty crowns per scalp and the captives were "sold for as much as they could agree with the purchasers."

John Gyles, a nine year old boy, was captured with his mother, Margaret, two sisters, Mary and Margaret, and a brother, James. He later wrote a memoir of his nine-year captivity by the Maliseets. His story is detailed in my book, *Terror on the Maine Frontier. The Ordeal and Triumph of John Gyles.*

The Kennebec settlements were now in the forefront of English intrusion into the lands of the Wabanaki Confederation.

Great Britain declared war on France in 1689, beginning The War of the League of Augsburg. American colonists called it King William's War. In the Dawnland the name of the war had no meaning, because the French, English and Natives had been in a nearly continual state of warfare. Sixteen hundred and eighty-nine was just a more violent year. Like all wars the general historical title meant nothing to the individuals fighting and dying on the ground and waters.

In May 1690 William Phips, who had been born in Pemaquid or Nequasset (now Woolwich) and acquired wealth salvaging a Spanish treasure ship, led a large expedition against Port Royal. Phips plundered the town and returned to Boston with captives and valuables, but it did little to stem the violence.

The Kennebec was the avenue for a French force of Canadians and Abenakis commanded by Captains Portneuf and Courtemanche. Meeting another force under Captain de Rouville on the Kennebec, they went on to Casco (Falmouth) and Fort Loyal (Portland). More than one hundred were killed and Captain Sylvanus Davis and others were brought captive to Quebec.

Mrs. Hannah Swarton (Swarnton) of Falmouth later provided testimony of her capture in May 1690. The Kennebec River was their route to Canada. "In our travels about the shores of Casco-bay, and through the country to Kennebeck, I was compelled to carry heavy burdens, and go at their pace or be killed at once." Swarton reported that summer and winter they traveled up and through the Kennebec region until they reached Canada and Quebec in February 1691. There she became friends with Margaret Stilson, who had been captured at Broad Cove in 1689. Hannah and her youngest son were redeemed in 1695, but a daughter and two sons remained in Canada until 1701.

Major Benjamin Church led a force into the Kennebec region in 1690. After skirmishing at Merrymeeting Bay, he led a force up the Androscoggin, retook the Pejepscot fort and forty miles up river he destroyed an Indian village killing twenty-one Abenaki and plundering the Indian village.

Traveling in captured sloops, Abenaki and French forces terrorized the fishermen and settlers along the coast of the Dawnland.

The English struck back later the next year. The Massachusetts legislature had directed the militia to "visit the enemy, French and Indians at their headquarters at Ameras-cogen, Pejepscot or any other plat." Once there, they were to set about "killing, destroying and utterly rooting out the enemy also as much as can be done to redeeming or recovering our captives in any place."

Major Church in 1691 led a force to Merrymeeting Bay where they found Laurel Hill, a native fortified village, inhabited on their approach by a few men and mostly women and children, who were quickly killed or captured, including the wives of Kancamagus and Warumbee. They did recover two English captives, before traveling upriver to "Ticonic" (Taconic), another Abenaki village on the Kennebec, where they killed twenty Indians, rescued seven prisoners and captured several including Norridgewock Sachem Moxus.

The Kennebecs then asked for a truce and a meeting at the mouth of the Kennebec. On November 29, 1691 the Natives agreed to return all their prisoners on May 1, 1692 and to maintain peace in a treaty signed by Moxus. It barely lasted three months.

In February the Kennebecs and other Abenakis raided York killing forty eight and capturing seventy-three.

The May 1, 1692, date for returning captives at Wells came and went. Then Moxus, a leader at Norridgewock, led another French/Abenaki raid on Wells on June 10. Massachusetts militia captain, James Converse, led a successful defense at the Storer Garrison

House, but Abenakis captured one Englishman and tortured him to death. Thereby encouraging the other settlers to fight on.

Later that year Converse led a force up the Kennebec to Taconic. The Indians retreated but Converse's force burned the Abenaki dwellings and corn stores.

Meanwhile the experiment of unifying the northeastern colonies under one governor fell apart when William and Mary seized the English throne. The English government then united Massachusetts, Maine and Plymouth under Governor William Phips.

The new governor returned to his birthplace, Pemaquid, to begin construction of a large stone fort, William Henry, garrisoned by sixty men commanded by Benjamin Church. This would relieve the pressure on the small garrison on the Kennebec and throw down the gauntlet to the French who claimed from the Penobscot to the Kennebec River.

The Kennebec and other Wabanaki tribes complained to the French governor, Comte de Frontenac, who promised swift action to remove the English east of the Kennebec. In 1693 Frontenac attacked the Iroquois in New York, but after an abortive expedition from Acadia the Dawnland was left in relative peace.

In the winter of 1693 Natives seized a sloop near Pemaquid killing the captain and wounding several crewmen. Church reported the Indians were "constantly stalking" the fort and its garrison and then the warriors seized a small sloop that had been sent out "to fetch wood for the Supply of the Fort."

With English garrisons at Pemaquid, Kennebec and Saco and no immediate military support from Canada, leaders of the Wabanakis journeyed to Pemaquid in August 1693 for another treaty conference.

Native leaders from Saco, Androscoggin, Kennebec and Penobscot tribes journeyed to Pemaquid.

The Norridgewock natives were represented by Wessembomet, Ketterramogis, Egremet and "Weenokoson of Teconnet". Madockawando and many others were there for the Penobscots.

John Wing, Nicholas Manning and Benjamin Jackson were there for the English governments.

The tribal leaders agreed "at all times and for ever, from and after the date of these presents we will cease and forbear all acts of hostility towards the subjects of the crown of England."

They agreed to "abandon and forsake the French interest" nor would they "succor or conceal any of the enemy Indians of Canada."

"All English captives in the hands or power of any of the Indians, within the limits aforesaid, shall with all possible speed be set at liberty, and returned home without any ransom or payment."

The Natives agreed that the English shall and may peaceably and quietly enter upon, improve and forever enjoy all and singular rights of lands, and former settlements and possessions within the eastern parts of the said province of Massachusetts Bay.

All trade would be controlled by Massachusetts and all disputes would be settled by English law.

To guarantee the Natives adherence to this treaty, Abassaonbamett, Egremet and Bagatawawongon aka Sheepscot John, were to be taken to Boston as hostages.

It is hard to believe that the Indigenous leaders understood all that they had promised without getting anything in return, not even a written promise of good behavior by the English negotiators.

Massachusetts even passed an act to regulate trade with the Indians in 1694 to provide truck houses for trade in accordance with this treaty. The province would provide money to buy supplies, restrict the sale of liquor and limit the sale of guns and ammunition to the quantity needed for hunting.

The act had a grandiose purpose according to the Massachusetts legislature: "Whereas the Indians within the Eastern part of this province, under the obedience of the Crown of England, have dependence upon the English for supplies of clothing and other necessaries, as formerly they have been accustomed, which that they may not want; and to the intent that the Christian religion be not scandalized, nor any injustice done to the Indians by extortion, in the taking of unreasonable or excessive prices for the goods sold unto them."

But it was too late. The Abenaki tribes had already rejoined with the French to force them out of the Dawnland.

Again, no English captives were returned and within a year the Wabanaki tribes were once more launching large scale attacks on the English settlements.

Hundreds of Norridgewock, Penobscot and Maliseet warriors led by Madockawando, Bomazeen and Claude Sebastien de Villieu rampaged across the Eastern District on their way to Oyster River, (now Durham, New Hampshire) which was destroyed on July 18, 1694 with the death of 104 English settlers and capture of 27 English settlers.

Early in 1695 Governor William Stoughton of Massachusetts threatened the Kennebecs and other Wabanakis with severe violence if they did not return all their captives. In the January 21, 1695, letter he called them "enemies of the crown of England " who were responsible for the "late tragical outrages and barbarous murders."

The Wabanaki reply, probably written by Jesuit Missionaries Sebastien Râle (Rale, Rasle) and Vincent Bigot who were at Norridgewock in 1695, rejected Stoughton s accusation.

Fathers Bigot and Râle helped rebuild the Abenaki village on the Kennebec previously occupied by the Indians who had moved to Canada after King Philip s War. Eventually the missionaries attracted three or four hundred Indians to Norridgewock. They accused the English of capturing warriors who had been carrying flags of parley. They denied exercising "any cruelty in killing thee only with hatchet blows and musket shots." They accused the English of "unparalleled treachery." They demanded the English "Bring or send us back my relatives whom thou detainest without cause. As for me, thou canst inflict much injury on me except by your treachery. My houses, my stores, my property are in inaccessible countries. If thou will confiscate them, they will cost thee a great deal of labor and fatigue." The challenges would soon be accepted.

Interestingly enough, Father Sebastien Râle, a missionary at Norridgewock in an April 15, 1693, letter to his Jesuit Superior, had described how the Abenaki tribesmen gloried in scalping their enemies and torturing their captives. "Still, this glory is even greater when they capture men alive. After tying them to a stake, "they heat their axes and gun barrels red hot and come one after the other to apply them now on one part of his body, now on another. Some take their lighted firebrands to burn him. Others slash him with their knives. These cut a piece of his flesh, already half roasted, and eat it in his presence." The priest added, "And the more the patient cries and suffers while they are applying these red hot irons to him the more he entertains the company."

John Gyles, a prisoner of the Maliseets, reported that in 1692 his brother James, a captive of the Penobscots, had been tortured, forced to eat his nose and ears, and burned at the stake for attempting to escape.

Life and death could be horrible on the Maine frontier.

After a year of relative peace, Toxus, a chief of the Norridgewock, Edgermet (Egeremet), another Kennebec chief, and Abenquid, a Penobscot chief, and several warriors appeared at Fort William Henry at Pemaquid on February 16, 1696.

The English version. The commander, Pascho Chubb, seeing a commotion between the Natives and some Englishmen, forcibly intervened. Egeremet and Abenquid with other Indians were killed as were at least two Englishmen.

The Native and French version. The Native leaders went to Pemaquid to begin negotiation for the return of the hostages held in Boston. The Natives and settlers traded and talked for several days, but then the English soldiers shot and killed Egermet and his son. A fight ensued where six Englishmen were killed and Toxus was rescued from the English soldiers. In the end four Natives were killed and six Englishmen. All due to "their treachery," according to a Capuchin priest, Father Thury, who had accompanied the Wabanakis to Pemaquid.

Toxus escaped with some warriors to return to the Kennebec. Not surprising, the Wabanaki tribes were not happy. Killing continued in remote areas of the Dawnland. That summer the French outfitted two armed sloops and carried Mi'kmaqs to Castine where they were joined by Penobscot warriors for a planned attack on Fort William Henry. Led by Baron St. Castin and Pierre LeMoyne D'Iberville hundreds of Wabanaki warriors including Kennebecs surrounded the fort and town of Jamestown on August 13. British army Captain Pasco Chubb

at first led a stout defense, but when the French brought in mortars and cannon Chubb surrendered despite his stonewalls and sixteen cannon. The French quickly took Chubb and his sixty soldiers to a nearby island to protect them from the Natives. Chubb was "universally censured," according to Râle. He was later jailed for cowardice but never brought to trial. The fort and the surrounding settlements were destroyed for the second time in less than a decade. Pemaquid s prominence as the easternmost English fortress in the Dawnland was over. It would be years before any number of settlers would return. Patrick Rodgers, one time commander of the fort at Georgetown, asserted there were few if any settlers east of the Kennebec. The French controlled Pemaquid until 1710 when General Francis Nicholson captured Nova Scotia and the Treaty of Utrecht confirmed English claims east of the Kennebec. But in 1696 the English settlements on the Kennebec now were the tip of English penetration into Wabanaki lands.

The Treaty of Ryswick in 1697 ended the war in Europe. France recognized William as the "legitimate" king of Great Britain. France gained the province of Alsace. In the American colonies all the territories were returned to their pre-war claimants. For Maine this meant that the land between the Kennebec River and Acadia was still claimed by the Abenaki tribes, the French and the English.

The French Governor General Villebon sought to reinforce their claim to the Kennebec in a September 5, 1698, letter to Lieutenant

Governor Stoughton and by sending missionaries to the Abenaki tribe at Norridgewock and constructing a chapel in the village.

In January 1699 the Wabanaki tribes reached a formal peace with Massachusetts. No settlers, fishermen or lumbermen were to live and work north of the Piscataqua River. Governor Richard Coote, Earl of Bellomont, complained to London: "All the Indians do not exceed 300 men fit to bear arms, yet this Province is said to have lost 1,000 families fit to bear arms." Probably an underestimation on the number of Abenaki and an overestimation on the English loss.

Later that year the Abenaki had to ask Bellomont to restore the truck house at Casco so they could obtain guns and supplies, in exchange for allowing fishermen in Casco Bay.

Later in 1699 the English led by Gyles and Major James Converse went "in a large Brigantine up the Kennebec , for Captives." In November the English returned to the Kennebec with annual gifts (bribes) for the Abenaki.

The British Lords of Trade recommended in a January 10, 1700, report that "Towards the mouth of the Kennebec River (seven leagues from Pemaquid) are many little Islands. On that of Damariscove there was before the war a Pallisaded Fort for the defense of the fishermen and another on Cape Nawagen where they use to cure their fishe. But to guard the Entrance of the River a Redoubt ought to be raised on the Island Sagadahock, and a little Fort at New Town in Rowseck [Arrowsic] Island, two leagues up the River where there was formerly a small square one Pallisaded."

After the death of Massachusetts Governor Phips, the English government tried once more to unite Massachusetts, New Hampshire, and New York under one governor, the Earl of Bellomont. He promptly warned the Board of Trade that the frontier forts "are in so Ruinous a Condition that they will now scarce bear the firing of a Gun upon them." But he was more interested in the New York frontier than the Eastern frontier.

The Earl of Bellomont promptly sent an emissary to Quebec to arrange for an exchange of prisoners and Indian captives. Governor

Frontenac refused. After his death the Governor called for a general exchange of prisoners. More than thirty tribes, including the Kennebecs showed up for the 1701 peace conference. All but the Iroquois brought their captives.

One wonders at what point the Wabanaki (Wulstukwiuks) tribal leaders began to realize that if either the French or the English came to dominate the Dawnland they had no future abilities to preserve their culture and way of life or even exist. The struggle for the Natives had become an existential one.

Both the English and the Natives realized that the status quo could not continue. Either the English must be forced out of more settlements as they had at Pemaquid or the English would resettle and expand the areas of settlement before the last war.

Joseph Dudley was appointed governor of Massachusetts by Queen Anne in 1702. He arrived in Boston on June 11. In his first speech to the Massachusetts General Court he urged them to rebuild the fort at Pemaquid and plan to capture Port Royal. The General Court did not agree.

The English were no longer as interested in the declining fur trade with the "Eastern Indians," but urged on by real estate speculators the English governments and pioneering families were certainly more interested in expanded English settlements. The lull after King William's War was short.

Queen Anne's War began in Europe in 1702 over the usual dynastic issues. Queen Anne declared war on France in May. Prince Phillipe of France became the king of Spain. England, Holland and the Holy Roman Empire tried to prevent it. After nine years of war they admitted failure.

Hostilities remained on the Eastern margins in 1702. Fisherman were kidnapped by Natives near Nova Scotia.

But the Kennebec region remained relatively peaceful until the summer of 1703. Then, as Samuel Penhallow, wrote:"there was no safety to him that went out, not him that came in, but dreadful calamity on every side."

Dudley went to Falmouth to meet with the Native leaders on June 20, 1703. The Penacooks, Sokolis, Anasagunticooks (Androscoggin), Norridgewock, Kennebecs and Penobscots were there.

Moxus and Hopgood represented the Norridgewock and Bomaseen and Capt. Samuel represented the Kennebecs. More than 250 Indians arrived in 65 canoes.

Dudley said he wished "to reconcile every difficulty, whatever, that has happened since the last treaty."

The Native leaders spoke of peace. Bomaseen and Samuel admitted that "several missionaries from the french, lately among them, had endeavored to break the union and seduce them from their allegiance to the crown of England, but had made no impressions on them, for they were as firm as the great rocks, and should continue so as long as the sun and moon endured."

At the conclusion of the treaty meeting, Penhallow concluded: "The eastern inhabitants who before had thoughts of removing, were now encouraged to stand their ground; several more were also preparing to settle among them, partly from the fertility of the soil, the plenty of timber, the advantage of fishery, and several other inducements."

All was but an illusion or treachery on the part of the French and Natives.

Never was that truer than fifty days later, when the French and Wabanaki tribes, including the Kennebec, descended on Wells and neighboring settlers in August 1703. Frontier warfare was becoming a cruel fact of life for Natives and English settlers.

Governor Phillipe Vaudreuil of Canada had decided to send a French force south under Alexandre Beaubassin, after Father Râle assured him that the Kennebecs at Norridgewock "were ready to take up the hatchet against the English whenever he gave them the order." He also later assured his nephew in an October 15, 1722, letter that "the Whole Abenaki is Christian and full of zeal for the maintenance of its religion." Despite the ease of acquiring goods and the cheapness of goods at nearby Cushnoc, the Indians, according to the good priest were attached to the French because of "this attachment to the Catholic faith."

Moxus, Wenongonet (Wenoggenet) and Sassacombunt led two hundred Kennebecs south with the French troops and Mi'kmaqs in an overwhelming attack on Wells, Saco and other English settlements west of the Kennebec.

According to later English reports the Kennebec sagamores approached under a flag of truce. When the English commander, John March, met at the parley, the English were suddenly attacked by the Natives. March was rescued but several of his men were killed.

The French and Native forces then burned houses and forts at Wells, Saco, Black Point, Casco (Falmouth), Spurwink (Cape Elizabeth) and Purpooduck (South Portland) between August 10 and 19. More than one hundred and fifty English settlers were killed or captured. At Casco they captured a sloop and two shallops to bolster their fleet of canoes.

Penhallow later wrote: "six weeks after," the Casco Treaty "the Eastern Country was in a flame, no house standing nor garrison unattackt. August 10 at 9 in the morning they began their bloody cruelty being 500 Indians with a number of french, dividing themselves into several small companies & made a descent on the several inhabitants from Casco to Wells at one and the same time, and spared none of whatever Age or Sex."

It was the Eastern Abenaki's last best chance to drive the English settlers beyond the Piscataqua River.

When the Abenaki were done, seventy-three persons were killed and ninety-five led into captivity.

Governor Dudley described the failure of the peace efforts of the English and the Natives attack to Governor Fitz-John Winthrop of Connecticut. "After all possible care an cost to quiet our Eastern Indians, which has lasted one year, they are now broken out and about 200 of them, with 20 French men, the last week fell in upon Wells, and the small settlements eastward; and have burnt and destroyed what they found distant from the garrisons, and have assaulted the forts at Saco Blackpoint and Casco but they are yet safe."

The English counterattacked in September and November with a force under Major March chasing some of the Wabanaki's back to Pigwacket (Fryeburg). Six Wabanakis were killed and six were captured. But on October 6 the Wabanaki warriors returned to Black Point, Spurwink, York and Purpooduck (the latter two now Cape Elizabeth) killing or capturing seventy-four English settlers. The garrison house at Black Point was burned.

The winter brought a brief respite, but the settlements were totally disrupted. As one English petitioner wrote to the Massachusetts leaders: We "have our Hands much taken from our Labours by Watching, Warding, Frequent Alarms."

He added: "Many of Us are driven from Our Homes. Much of our stock is killed by the Heathen; Many of Our able Men removed from Us, and Many thinking of Moveing if they knew wither to goe…and Wee daily grow more & more feeble and deplorable: daily Walking and working with Fear, Trembling & Jeopardy of Life."

Motivated by increased bounties of £10 an adult Indian captive or scalp and £20 for a captive Native child ten or under, English Indian hunters unsuccessfully roamed the woods during the winter, but they at least kept the Abenaki on their toes.

The Abenaki had their warriors and the English had their Indian hunters.

The Abenaki then turned their attention to Massachusetts destroying the outlying town of Deerfield on February 28, 1704.

That about sums up the condition of the interactions of English settlers and Natives in the Dawnland.

In the spring Massachusetts reinforced its eastern garrison houses with additional troops and the addition of Pequot and Mohegan warriors from Connecticut.

The Kennebecs and other Wabanaki tribes were not intimidated, killing and capturing several settlers in Maine.

Colonel Benjamin Church attacked the Abenakis of the Dawnland in the early summer of 1704. Stopping at the Kennebec along their way to Penobscot and Aadia they killed and captured several Wabanaki before reaching the Bay of Fundy where they burned the French towns of Grande Pré and Port Royal. Although they decided against attacking the fort of Port Royal they returned to Boston in three months with over one hundred French and Native prisoners, including the Abenaki daughter of Baron de Saint Castin.

The next year Governor Vaudreuil and Massachusetts Governor Dudley opened negotiations for peace with an exchange of prisoners. The French held 117 and the Natives held at least 60, but when the exchange occurred the French could only muster 60 at Quebec to exchange for 70 from Massachusetts.

Most of the fighting during the ten years of Queen Anne's War was not around the Kennebec. The British made several attempts to capture Quebec and Port Royal in Acadia. Finally on the third attempt at Port Royal in 1710 the British captured Port Royal. French privateers ravaged the coast of the Eastern District capturing hundreds of fishing vessels. The Abenaki tribes fought the English west of the Kennebec in what is now southern Maine and New Hampshire. The Abenaki joined other tribes in raids in the Massachusetts towns of Deerfield (1704) and Groton (1707). Wells, Falmouth and Casco Bay saw numerous Abenaki raids.

Samuel Moody reported to Joseph Dudley on January 27, 1709/10 that the Abenaki "of Kennebeck had been quiet above a year, and designed to remain so, but withal cautioned him to be very carefull, for they believ'd the French Indians would be abroad & do all the Mischief they could."

Jared Dudley told the English Board of Trade in a December 2, 1712, letter that the "Indians have committed barbarous murders and Burnt many Houses in Company with the French and their Dependant Indians."

However, he was sure the "Kennebecks, Penobscot & Norigwock" are "weary of the Warr having Lost some Hundreds of their Number and are not now left above three or four Hundred men."

Indeed the Eastern Abenaki made peace with the Massahusetts government in July 1713.

According to recent historians, such as Ian Saxine, there were about 500 Abenakis on the Kennebec, concentrated at Norridgewock. There were also small numbers of Abenaki in the villages of Amaseconti and Naracomigog on the upper Kennebec and the Androscoggin rivers. Estimated numbers ran as high as 2,500 with 900 at St. François (St. Francis) and Becancour (Wowenock, 750 on the Penobscot and 400 Mi kmaqs at Meductic on the St, John River. However, we shall see that contemporaries, such as John Gyles, put the number much lower.

The Treaty of Utrecht brought Hudson Bay, Acadia and Newfoundland into British rule, leaving only Cape Breton and Prince Edward Islands, along with the St. Lawrence River Valley in French Hands.

Abenaki sachems sought a peace conference at Portsmouth in July 1713. Twenty Massachusetts and New Hampshire representatives showed up at Portsmouth. Delegates from the St. John (Maliseet), Kennebec and Penobscot tribes were represented. The Saco, Merrimack and Androscoggin were not. Warraeensat, Wadacanquan and Bomaseen were there for the Kennebecs.

In the treaty the "Natives conceded claims to all the settled lands but all agreed that the Natives controlled "their lands" with "the Liberty of hunting, fishing and fowling, and all other lawful liberties and privileges as enjoyed on the 11 of August, 1693.

The New England governments were to regulate trade and truck houses and the Indians agreed to never trade at any other places.

Both sides agreed all controversies would be settled by English law and justice.

The treaty was then brought to Casco, where Moxus led a large group of Natives who signaled their agreement to the treaty "by loud huzzas, of acclamations of joy" and the acceptance of presents.

The treaty gave all participants a chance to regroup and regain strength both on the Kennebec and in Europe.

Both sides had suffered severe losses during the ten years. It was estimated that more than one-fourth of the English settlers in Maine were killed, captured or simply moved out.

Contemporary estimates put the Indian losses at one third of the population. According to Williamson there were about 300 Abenaki and Mi kmaq. The Wawenocks, Sokolis and Anasgunticooks were decimated by losses or migrations to Canada. More recent estimates of Natives are more generous. Ian Saxine estimates there were about 900 Abenaki at St. François and Becancour, 750 Penobscots and 500 Kennebecs.

Wabanakis had two villages on the Kennebec River–Norridgewock and further up the river, Amaseconti.

This might have lessened the conflicts on the Kennebec but misunderstandings and simple violations of the treaty in the years following only increased tensions and conflict.

CHAPTER THREE
RIVER RUNS RED

After the Treaty of Utrecht in 1713, settlers headed north to the Eastern District. The Pejepscot Proprietors headed by Thomas Hutchinson, father of Governor Thomas Hutchinson, purchased the claims of Thomas Purchase and Richard Wharton in the area of Merrymeeting Bay and the Androscoggin and Kennebec rivers. The company offered free transportation and five-year tax exemptions. Many settlers took up the offer and wandered eastward across the bay to the Kennebec.

At this time the population of Massachusetts has been estimated at around 96,000 and New Hampshire at 9,650. Many were looking for landed opportunities along the coast of the Eastern District. Most of the English settlers in the Dawnland came from these two provinces.

The "re-settlement" of the lower Kennebec centered on Arrowsic (Arrowsick, Arroseg), because of its access to both the ocean and the Kennebec. Arrowsic was also one of the five towns in the Eastern District approved for resettlement by the Massachusetts General Court's "Committee of Eastern Claims and Settlement" in 1713. Saco, Scarborough, Falmouth and North Yarmouth were the others. The committee was authorized to settle claims for abandoned lands and buildings.

The General Court required resettlement by at least twenty families. Every family was to have three to four acres and each village was to build a defensible garrison house.

On the whole, settlers ignored the General Court's requirements and they haphazardly returned without approval or organization. Timber pirates cruised the coast cutting the best timber and mast trees without any pretense to ownership of the land. The Committee of Eastern Claims did its best, but the frontier people were for the most part uncontrollable.

John Watts, a member of the Pejepscot Company, and twenty families came to Arrowsic in 1714. John Higginson, John Watts and Biby Lake promptly petitioned the Massachusetts General Court to allow "them a company of men to be a security for the people in their settlement of a Town of Forty Families." The General Court saw the settlement at Arrowsic as "a Barrier & Security to the other Four" towns southwest of the Kennebec.

The General Court on October 29, 1714 directed the governor "to order a sergeant with nineteen centinels from the Fort at Casco Bay to Arrowsic Island to continue there for the space of six months to cover and defend the designed settlement."

The province also established truck houses there and at the mouth of the Saco.

Two years later Hutchinson and John Gerrish and "the first settlers on Arrowsic Island prayed that an addition may be made to their number of men, or at least to continue the twenty-six men now there." The petitioners also asked to form a township named Georgetown. The General Court agreed to continue sixteen men in the public pay "at Arrowsic Island now denominated Georgetown."

The Committee of Eastern Claims in 1715 accepted the plans of the Pejepscot Company (Proprietors) for new settlements at Brunswick and Topsham.

And so on the other side of Merrymeeting Bay, the Pejepscot Company was building a new fort– Fort George to be built and commanded by Captain John Gyles, who had survived nine-years as an enslaved captive of the Maliseets. Fort George was built on the ashes of Fort Andros which had been burned by the Norridgewock tribe and French in 1694.

Gyles had just begun work when "the Indians came in the night, and forbade our laying one stone upon another. I told them I came with orders from Governor Dudley to build a fort, and if they disliked it, they might acquaint him with it; and that if they came forcibly upon us, they or I should fall on the spot. After such hot words they left us, and we went on with our building, and finished it November 15, 1715"

In his many reports, Gyles warned the governor that Iroquois and Canadian Indians were trying to convince the local Abenakis on the Androscoggin and Kennebec rivers to join them in a renewed war against the English. "Thier is great motions among the Indians the Carolina Indians and the Mohox sending belts of Peque [wampum] to our Indians to know if they would Joyn with them upon occasion which they have as yet Refused the belts & Denied to concern in Trouble as to a Warr". The Mohawk grievance, reported Gyles, was the killing of a Mohawk Sagamore by the English at Albany. They are expecting war this summer, and hope to convince "these Eastward Indians" to join them against the English. "I indevor to make our Indians sensible that it is all falce and Delusions from those furronors and intrigue to bring them into trouble."

The Kennebecs tried to enlist more aid from the French in repelling the settlers, but they were disappointed when French Governor de Vaudreuil only promised to send arms and ammunition in secret. The Kennebecs mocked the French help: exclaiming "Is this how a father helps his children." When Vaudreuil offered to get the support of other tribes, the Kennebec delegation reportedly responded with "mocking laughter." In truth both the French and Natives were confronted with a growing tide of English settlers-arriving not individually but in groups with the backing of wealthy proprietors.

Continued Indian hostilities and settlers' encroachment on Native lands up the Kennebec brought Governor Samuel Shute to Arrowsic on August 9-12, 1717 to convince the Wabanakis to allow the English to live on the lower Kennebec. Leaders from the Kennebec, Penobscot, Saco, Pigwacket and Mi'kmaq tribes attended.

Many of the settlers in Maine were in violation of the 1713 Treaty of Portsmouth that restricted English settlements east of the Saco River. The Kennebec sachem Wiwurna told Shute in no uncertain terms that the Wabanaki wanted the forts and settlements along the Kennebec removed. The governor asserted that the Natives had sold their land along the Kennebec River and that the tribal leaders "must desist from any Pretentions to lands which the English own."

The Abenaki insisted they must not be molested on their lands and protested against any further forts or settlements beyond Pemaquid. A long retreat from the earlier red lines of the Saco and then the Kennebec.

Speaking for the Kennebecs, Chief Wiwurna who would later be killed at Norridgewock when the river ran red with blood, told Governor Shute–this is "our lands."

"This place was formerly settled and is now settling at our request and we now return thanks that the English are come to settle here, and will embrace them in our bosoms that come to settle our lands."

Governor Shute then replied: "They must not call it their land, for the English have bought it of them and their ancestors."

Wiwurna then answered Shute: We pray leave to proceed in our answer, and talk of this matter afterward. We desire there may be no more settlements made. We shan't be able to hold them all in our bosoms, and to take care and shelter them, if it be bad weather and mischief is threatened. We are willing to cut off our lands as far as the mills (on the Kennebec) and the coasts to Pemaquid."

Governor Shute then contradicted Wiwurna: "Tell them we desire only what is our own, and that we will have. We will not wrong them, but what is our own we will be masters of."

Wiwurna then protests recalling a previous treaty: "It was said at Casco Treaty, that no more forts should be made."

Shute then replied: "Tell them that the forts are not made for their hurt, and that I wonder they should speak against them, when they are for the security of both, we being all subjects of King George. King George builds what forts he pleases in his own dominions, and has given me power to do it here, and they are for their security as well as ours, and the French do the like. They build what forts they [want] and all kings have that power, and the governors they appoint do the same."

Wiwurna then countered: "We can't understand how our lands have been purchased, what has been alienated was by our gift."

Wiwurna continued his claim: "As for the west side of the Kennebec river, I have nothing to say but I am sure nothing has been sold on the east side."

Governor Shute rejected that claim: "I expect their positive answer and compliance in this matter, that the English may be quiet in the possession of the lands they have purchased."

Wiwurna persisted: "We don't know what to think of the new forts built. We should be pleased with King George if there was never a fort in the eastern part."

Ultimately, the Wabanakis agreed to accept the illegal settlements if a new boundary was drawn and accepted. Shute replied "We desire only what is our own, and that we will have." Shute insisted they could build forts where they pleased and that the forts were for the protection of all "not for their hurt."

Not surprisingly, the Wabanakis were not satisfied.

After four days the conference ended with both sides pledging peace and amity, but clearly not understanding the assertions of each other. They spoke, but they did not hear.

The Kennebecs were still soliciting help from the French to defend them against the English "as we are not Eble to hindar their settling."

Vaudreuil told the Wabanakis "you were betrayed & Destroid by the English, I advise you to hendar their settling your Lands. I am informed their ar many settling."

Gyles told Shute that in a December 20, 1718, letter: "The Indians answer father Vodrell we ar well & ar not afraid of the English Hurting us, & we ar not Eble to hindar their settling they ar many in number, and so ar you therefore hender your Egels for your Kings ar Brothers & talk freely therefore Desiear him to order not to Settle our Lands, & you will oblige Us in hindering them though we Did till the English com half ways from Sacatahock to nasrangowock (Norridgewock)." In short, the Kennebecs feared that they could not prevent the English from moving eastward from the Saco to the Kennebec and beyond to the north and the east..

But at this point in time Gyles happily reported that "Our Indians hear seem to be very friendly & all their hunting & fishing as formerly," despite the "Many sendings from & to a sort of Indian to the westward of Albany & so Round to Canady but don't find they have brought Eany thing to Pass."

As if in response, Governor Shute encouraged the immigration of Scotch-Irish to the Eastern District of Massachusetts. By 1720, fifteen more families from Northern Ireland and England had arrived and the Natives were more uneasy.

Among them was Samuel Denny, who joined the Robinsons at Newtown (later Fort Menaskoux), across the river from the present town of Phippsburg. Denny and his sister Deborah had come to Boston from Combs, Suffolk County, England. Deborah married the Reverend Thomas Prince and Denny came to Arrowsic in 1719.

Denny and Robinson, who also came from Combs, opened a trading house inside a blockhouse. With his slaves for laborers, Denny had a thriving farm and business. While they were building it, a Kennebec warrior shot a man who was shingling the roof.

Because of these Indian raids, the Massachusetts government and the Pejepscot Proprietors in 1719-1720 built Fort Richmond (now Richmond) on the western side of the Kennebec River at the site of the truck house. The wooden fort surrounded by a stockade contained a blockhouse, truck house, chapel and quarters for officers and men. Captain Joseph Heath was the first commander.

At Merrymeeting Bay, Captain Gyles, who married Heath's daughter, Hannah, reported that the Natives were busy planting corn and catching fish. "I find nothing New amongst them they ar Generly to their fishing & following a Long they see the shoar as author years to such tim their Corn is hettable." Gyles cautioned that war rumors stir in Canada: "Sum Leatly from Canady say they wear Casioned to be Careful of the English yet they wear not insneared & trapped, & as yet send Powdar as Present to the Penobscot tribe."

Gyles added that local sagamore Bomazeen, described by Gyles as "a great Roge much Empowered by the French," nevertheless got a pass to go to Boston to collect gifts with "the approbation of their chiefs of narangowock [Norridgewock]. "

English militia captains, John Gyles, Jabez Bradbury, Joseph Bean(Bane) and Samuel Jordan, had spent years interacting with the Kennebecs. They often traveled up the river, scouting, mapping and even befriending the Natives. One Native later described Gyles "as a Captain of the Tribes in our Parts." All to no avail.

Edward Hutchinson reinforced Gyles' report of the peaceful nature of the local Indians, in a September 7, 1719, letter to Shute. The Indians from Norridgewock "seem dissatisfied that people should settle in a Body." On a local level at Georgetown, two Indians employed by a tenant farmer at Swan Island killed one of his oxen.

The Kennebec was the quickest trade and military route to Canada, and its upper reaches by way of the Sebasticook River the best route to the Penobscot. Norridgewock village, near the mouth of the Sandy River, was the key to controlling the river. The English were moving up from the coast and the French and their Native allies were trying to hold them at bay.

At another conference in 1720 the Wabanakis promised to pay restitution for the property they had destroyed in Maine and left four hostages in Boston until the restitution was paid.

John Wheelwright reported from Georgetown on August 10, 1720 that the Indians at Arrowsic "seem Very Inclinable to make a Warr."

The Kennebecs' concern continued over "a multitude of New Inhabitants," was plain even to Samuel Sewall, a member of the conference, who warned the Massachusetts Council in a September 8, 1721, letter. Rather than encouraging caution, it stimulated more aggression from the English settlers and government.

The Wabanaki leaders tried to do their part to keep peace, but were caught between their angry tribal members and the ever growing menace of English settlers and soldiers. Forts Richmond, St. Georges and George may have been seen as peacekeepers to the English, but they were just more threats to the Kennebec and other Abenaki tribes.

In 1721 the Wabanakis delivered two hundred of the four hundred promised beaver pelts and demanded the return of the hostages.

The Norridgewock tribe in May 1721 held a large meeting at their main village on the Kennebec to select a new chief to replace the recently deceased Toxus. The peace/conciliatory Natives chose Omkouiroumenit, a conciliatory, as sagamore. The Norridgewock then gave the English the remaining 200 promised beaver skins and promised to send four hostages to Boston to assure their good peaceful actions.

Moody reported to Shute on June 5 and 19, 1721 that the Norridgewock tribe had held a meeting and they plan to "bring their Skins hither & peremptorily to demand their hostages" and "insolently charge the Governmt with Folly in making New Demands."

Governor Vaudreuil told the Norridgewock they had been duped by the English. To Father Râle, he wrote: "the faint hearts of your Indians in giving hostages for damages done those, who would drive them from their native country, have convinced me, that the present is a crisis in which a moment is not to be lost.

Therefore, I have applied to the villages of St. Francois and Becancourt, and prevailed upon them to support with vigor their brethren Norridgewock, and send a deputation to the place appointed for negotiating the proposed treaty, who dare let the

English know, they will have to deal with other tribes than the one at Norridgewock, if they continue their encroachments." he had begun among them."

Vaudreuil sent another Jesuit, De la Chase and a Lieutenant de Croisel to Norridgewock to bolster the French interest.

At the beginning of August, two hundred Natives in ninety canoes, led by Father Râle and La Chase, Castin, and Croisel appeared at Georgetown. Landing at Padeshal s Island, they proceeded on to Arrowsic and handed Captain Penhallow a letter to Governor Shute. "If the settlers did not remove in three weeks," the letter declared, "the Indians would come and kill them all, destroy their cattle and burn their houses."

"You Englishmen have taken away the lands which the Great God has given our fathers and us," charged the Sagamores.

Hutchinson later wrote Râle who "was constantly, instigating them to insult and annoy the new settlers, whom he pretended, encroached upon the lands of the Indians, and by supplying them with strong drink debauched their morals and prevented the progress of the good work he had begun among them."

In the summer the four Norridgewock hostages in Boston escaped. Even though they were recaptured, reprisals were demanded. According to Father Râle, the Abenaki "bitterly complained that the law of nations, should be so violated in the midst of the peace which was enjoyed."

Shute and the Massachusetts General Court in August charged the Natives with "rebellion" and then demanded that the Natives hand over their priest, Father Sebastien Râle whom they described as "among the most infamous villains,", and any other Jesuits in their village. The Wabanakis refused and the raids continued.

Massachusetts then sent a sloop to the Penobscot River and seized Castin, the eldest son of Baron Jean de Castin and brought him to Boston. Although he was wearing a French army uniform, Castin told a committee of the General Court that he wanted to live in peace and explained why he had gone to Arrrowsic. "I have always lived with my kindred and people, my mother was one of them. I had command of them, and would not fail to attend a meeting where their interests were at stake. But I received no orders from Vaudreuil to attend. My habit is only an uniform suited to my birth and condition, for I have the honor of being an officer under the French King." Castin was allowed to return home.

The General Court in November resolved to prosecute the war against the "Eastern Indians for their many breaches of covenant." Colonel Thomas Westbrook was ordered to go to Norridgewock and seize Râle. The Council offered a reward of £200 for his capture.

In January 1721/ 22, a Massachusetts militia force under the command of Colonel Thomas Westbrook, but in actuality led by Captains Johnson Harmon and Joseph Heath, who had surveyed the land around Norridgewock, attacked Norridgewock on the Kennebec, but the Natives were not there.

Harmon and Heath described the raid in a January 21, 1721, letter to Colonel Edmund Goffe, commander of the Massachusetts forces sent against the Anbenaki tribes. Goffe was later accused of fraud, and forced to resign in 1724.

Harmon and Heath selected "Fifty Able Souldiers" and marched along the Kennebec to Norridgewock. "Tho the Jesuit (thro the inadvertancy of some) was Informed that we were preparing to give him a visit; yet that report did not gain his belief, but he remained sound until" an Indian warned him before they could reach him because the Indian was wearing snowshoes and Harmon's men did not. Harmon and Heath recommended they should "Imploy our Four hostages to make a quantity of good Indian snow shoes & mogasins."

"The Jesuit was not removed to Canada according to the Indian report to us neither was he out of his house many hours before we were in it. For because the weather was exceedingly cold & no fire place in it, yet neither his Ink in his stand or Drink in his pot were froz'd."

They continued: "The Jesuit was well provided with good things for house lodging, beside a considerable quantity of furs, but considering him as a Subject to a Prince, with whom his Brittanick Majesty is at peace, and lest the Jesuit should animate his Indians to make reprizal upon the Frontier people by killing their Cattle we left all his effects intire Excepting his Papers which we have herewith sent you, supposing they will give the Governt a True light of Him & those yet Countenance his designs."

"We are of opinion that the Jesuit is returned to Norridgewalk by this time, & will be made secure as if we had not marched thither, supposing there will be no more attempts against him this winter and therefore we believe he may yet be taken this winter if proper methods be taken. But its vain to attempt it Except the Affair be kept secret & able men chose & well provided with good snow shoes & moginsons so they may be very Expeditious in the march. The Souldiers in the Frontier seem very willing to go again if they may be well fitted out."

Harmon and Heath added a description of the chapel: "The Meeting House at Norridgwalk is a large handsome Logg Building adorned within with many Pictures & Toys to please the Indians, which we found them very fond of, & afraid we would deface," but they did not.

The *New England Courant* printed a report on Colonel Thomas Westbrook's raid in its February 12, 1721/22 issue: "Last week his Excellency received a Letter from the Forces at the Eastward, giving an Account, that as they were marching to seize Father Ralle, he made his Escape out of the House with so much haste that (being then writing) he left his Papers on the Table, among which was found a Letter from the Governor of Canada, directing the Indians to use their utmost Force, to keep the English from settling at the Eastward, and promising to supply them with Powder and Ball for that End, at the same Time charging the Jesuit to keep the matter Private. 'Tis said his Excellency has wrote to England of this Affair."

Harmon and Heath took the strong box, the chapel bell and crucifix, and probably most importantly to Father Râle the Indian dictionary that he had been building for years. The chapel bell and strong box are now at the Maine Historical Society.

Correspondence in the captured strong box implicated the French and the Jesuits in inciting the Norridgewock Tribe to violence against the settlers, fueling English anger toward the Kennebecs.

Father Râle described his escape in his October 1722 letter to his nephew. "I had remained alone in the village with a small number of old and infirm people, while the rest of the savages were at the chase. This time appeared favourable for surprising me, and with this purpose they sent a detachment of two hundred men. Two young Abenakis who were hunting along the seashore learned that the English had entered the river. Immediately they turned their steps in that direction to observe their march." Having been warned the missionary "had only time to swallow the consecrated wafers and to pack in a little box the sacred vessels, and to make my escape to the woods." The English soldiers "came within eight paces of the tree which covered me," but did not discover him. "Thus by a special protection of God, I escaped their hands. They pillaged my church and my little house."

The raid on Norridgewock also angered the Wabanakis and brought more Indian attacks on the settlements.

"These reiterated insults," according to the missionary, "drove our savages to the conclusion that they had no more answer to look for, and that it was time to repel violence and to make open force succeed to pacific negotiations. On their return from the chase and after having put their seed into the ground they took the resolution to destroy the English habitations recently constructed and to remove to a distance from their abodes those restless and formidable neighbors, who little by little were gaining a foothold upon their lands and were planning to reduce them to slavery.

They sent a deputation into different villages of the savages to get them interested in their cause and to engage them to lend a hand under the necessity that was upon them of making a just defense. The deputation had its success. The war song was chanted among the Hurons of Lorette and in all the villages of the Abenaki nation. Nabrabtsouak was the place appointed for the assembling of the warriors in order that they might agree together upon the plan of operations.

In the meantime the Nanrantsouakians moved down the river; arriving at its mouth they took away three or four little buildings of the English. Then coming up the same river, they pillaged and burnt the new house which the English had built. They nevertheless abstained from all the violence toward the inhabitants, they even allowed them to depart their homes with the exception of five whom they kept as hostages till their compatriots detained in the prisons of Boston should be restored to them. This moderation of the savages did not have the effect which they had hoped. On the contrary an English party, having found sixteen Abenakis asleep on an island, opened a general fire upon them by which five of them were killed and three wounded.

Thus we have a new signal of the war which is likely to flame forth between the English and the savages. The latter look for no support from the French, by reason of the peace which reigns between the two nations; but they have a resource in all the other savage nations, who will not fail to enter into their quarrel and to take up their defense."

That summer Governor Shute warned Governor Vaudreuil that Father Râle was violating English territory. "As to Monsieur Ralle s Mission among the Indians I shall be glad, if by his preaching he has brought those poor Savages any thing nearer to the Kingdom of Heaven, than they were before he went thither; But that which I have to say to him, and to you upon his Account is, that Norridgewack the seat of his Mission is within the Territory of His Majesty King George, and that it is contrary to an Act of Parliament of Great Britain and a law of this Province for a Jesuit or Romish Priest to Preach or even reside in any part of the British Dominions."

During the winter Governor Shute resigned his post and returned to England, before the English could successfully rid themselves of this "Romish Priest."

The Indigenous People were frustrated with the English settlers' determination to increase their land holdings and mount larger raids against their villages. They accused the English of cheating them in trade and providing "flaming" liquor. The French, they frequently said, gave them presents and religion and did not take their land. The French welcomed them in Canada, but the Indians did not want to go. As the English failed to honor the boundary lines pledged in treaties, the Indians plaintively asked: "Whither should we go?"

On March 25, 1722 eleven Indians appeared at Richmond and shot one soldier, according to Samuel Shute.

In the summer of 1722 "calamity" soon became the norm on the Kennebec, according to Captain John Penhallow, commander at Georgetown and son of Samuel Penhallow.

Captain Penhallow, reported to Governor Shute on June 15, 1722, that the Kennebecs were causing death, destruction and pandamonium on the Kennebec and at Merrymeeting Bay.

"The common calamity of this part of the country is such that the people on the river [Kennebec] and Merrymeeting Bay are all flying for shelter, and that no arguments can persuade them to keep their houses, at least for the present. The Indians began their hostilities upon nine or ten families and took such a number of 'em as they thought fit. They used 'em very barbarously–burning their houses at midnight, hauling 'em out of bed by the hair, and striped 'em of whatever was valuable. Those they gave liberty to go away, they left hardly anything to cover them. About thirty people they have already treated thus. Yesterday morning they killed ten oxen belonging to Mr. Alexander Hamilton and Broens, and some others of their cattle, and carried away only the fat of their inwards. They make great spoil of cattle and let their flesh lye on the ground.

They have burnt Mr. [Robert] Temple's house at the chops of the bay, and killed some of his cattle—cut all the canoes to pieces that they met with there. In short, they have done what they pleased in Merrymeeting Bay and upon this river, and have endeavored for some days (which we have since discovered) of surprising the whale boats that meet in Merrymeeting Bay to give intelligence from place to place, and to discover the Indians. The boats had parted but a few hours before they began their hostilities upon the inhabitants. I trust your Excellency has express by land of this matter, so that I have only to enclose a letter I received from one of the captives by one of the subscribers they set at liberty.

We shall keep on our cruises with the whale boats; am also sending out about twenty men in two or three boats, to save what cattle the Indians had left perishing on the ground."

The Abenaki rounded up the nine families living on Point Pleasant, but kept only five to exchange for three Indians being held captive. Zacheriah Trescott, Alexander Hamilton, Hansard, Robert Love and Henry Edgar were first brought to Norridgewock and then moved on to Canada. Trescott wrote Dudley from Canada on October 1, 1722, that if the governor would "send the three naregwock Indiens and they will let us 5 go free." Trescott and Hansard were not freed until November 1724 and they returned to Merrymeeting Bay.

Henry Edgar's wife Jane and James Watt's wife Maragaret petitioned the General Court on September 3, 1723, "shewing that both their husbands are captives of the Indian enemy, and that Seven of their Children are also in Captivity. That there is an Indian woman named Elizabeth with her children now in the hands of this Government, and they pray that their husbands and children be exchanged for Elizabeth and her children." The house dismissed the petition. What happened to the children and James Watt is not known.

Edgar was ransomed in late 1724 and moved to Gloucester.

Hamilton returned in 1723 and went to the Kennebec. Love, also, returned in early 1723 and asked the General Court to repay Peter Schuyler £75.7.3 for his ransom and expenses.

The Boston jail still held nine Indians in 1727.

At nearly the same time sixty warriors in twenty canoes attacked Fort St. Georges (now Thomaston) on June 15, 1722, "where they burnt a sloop" and "took several prisoners." Twenty settlers and five Wabanakis were killed. The Eastern Wabanakis then moved down the coast to Damariscove and Broad Bay (Bremen) destroying isolated houses on their way to the Kennebec where they joined the local Kennebecs.

Captain Gyles, commander of Fort George, in a separate letter added that on July 1, 1722: "A number of Indians engag'd Fort George about two hours, kill'd one Person and then drew off to Killing Cattle etc."

The Abenakis then moved across Merrymeeting Bay to the settlements on Arrowsic and the lower Kennebec.

On July 4, 1722, the Abenakis attacked Denny's blockhouse, where the settlers were attending a church service. One child was the only death, but twenty-six houses were burned and about fifty cattle were killed. According to Reed in his history of Bath, those houses were never rebuilt.

John Penhallow, commander of the fort on the lower Arrowsic described the attack in a letter to Governor Shute. "I rec'd yr Excys Letter of Express of the 20th ult. But last night, this morning, I Dispatched away my whale boat up the river & called in the Inhabitants. I also ordered the Boat to Richmond to direct the officer there to keep good Guards inasmuch as I had but just heard of Capt. Westbrooks being attacked at St. Georges etc. the Damage that was done there, but as soon as the Boat had got as far as Merrymeeting Bay they saw about 30 of the Indians, who as soon as they found themselves Discovered man'd out their Canoos in chase of the Boat wch was then obliged to return & soon got Clear of them, the Houses in the Bay were Just then Sat on fire, &

after the Boat returned to me, wth the above ac[coun]t we observed smokes to rise in Long Reach & mr Allen, the bearer being at his own House about three mile of, I was willing to try to Save him, & Immediately man'd out the Boat wth fresh hands & relieved him, who had been in defence of his House about two hours, it happened we did not Loose a man, tho they fought the Indians about half an hour before they could get Mr. Allen away, it's probable our men wounded if not killed Some of the Indians.

There is five Garrisons in this Town but can keep but three wch will defend one another & we are in a good Posture of Defence.

I am further strengthening in according to your Excels order, they are within Shot of one another & some good Houses between that we are able to receive and Entertain a good number of men. Mr. Allen who now comes up will give your Excy, a more particular act. of his loss & what happened to him this day. I have divided my half Com[ma]nd, that are here, among the three Garrisons for their better Defence, am fortifying for the Security of the Stores, would pray yr Excy to order me two Swivil Guns to fix in the flankers for the Security of the Same, there and here Several Lusty Young men that have been robbed of all they had by the Indians, who would be glad of service if yr Excy would be pleased to admit of it, they Cannot possibly Subsist here without. I have detained em till yr Excy, order inasmuch as their going off now will weaken the County."

On July 25, Shute formally declared war on the Wabanakis, particularly the Kennebecs at Norridgewock. Dummer's War or Râle s War had begun in earnest.

The danger on Arrowsic was high that summer, and bloodshed came again on September 10, 1722. About twenty farmers lived on Arrowsic in 1722, under the protection of a fort commanded by John Penhallow. As was regularly done, the garrison sent a small group of soldiers out on September 10 to protect the farmers harvesting their crops. That day the soldiers spotted Kennebec and St. Francis warriors in the woods, and fired on them killing one and wounding three. The soldiers and settlers then retreated to the fort/

garrison house. The Abenakis attacked the fort and killed Samuel Broaking through a porthole. After looting and burning twenty-six houses and killing cattle, the natives from Norridgewock retreated to the woods, where 70 neighboring settlers commanded by Colonel Walton and Captain Johnson Harmon (Harman) caught up to them. The English force was fought off by the Natives, who then took to their canoes and a captured English sloop. They returned to Norridgewock but not before briefly attacking Fort Richmond, commanded by Captain Joseph Heath. Failing to breach the fort the warriors burned houses and killed cattle.

Colonel Thomas Westbrook led a Massachusetts fleet and small army in March 1723 against the Penobscot fort on the Penobscot River. But when they arrived the Natives were not there. Perhaps they had fled. Perhaps they were still in their winter villages in the interior. Westbrook burned the vacant buildings and food supplies.

At the same time Captain Johnson Harmon led a small force up the Kennebec to the Native village of Norridgewock at Old Point, but they failed to mount a direct attack, blaming weak ice on the river. Dummer told Harmon on March 8, 1722/23 that he understood "the openness of the Rivers & the Wetness of the Country rendered the Execution of my Orders for a march to Wedembeseck & Norridgewock impracticable." But he was to continue the armed scouting parties.

Harmon was a veteran of Indian attacks. As a child he had helped fight off attacks at York and Winter Harbour (Biddeford). In 1710 Harmon had been taken prisoner by Bomazeen and was later exchanged for Beauvenire de Vercheres on May 22, 1711. The death of his parents and his captivity fueled Harmon's anger, perhaps even hatred toward the Wabanakis.

In September 1723 Capt. Joseph Heath, commander at Fort Richmond, led a small force north against the French and Indians. Although somewhat inconsequential, two English soldiers John Green and Joseph Anderson petitioned the General Court for support claiming they could not support themselves. Green had been shot that "carried away his left cheek and part of his Jaw-bone." Joseph Anderson lost fingers on both of his hands. Even small clashes brought disaster to some participants.

In return the Wabanaki Confederation warriors besieged the small force at Fort St.Georges in December, 1723 for thirty days. However, they held out until a rescue force under Colonel Westbrook broke the siege. Severe damage was done to the surrounding dwellings and cattle.

The Wabanaki from the Kennebec joined in small raids at Scarborough, Berwick and Cape Porpoise (now Kennebunkport).

The Wabanaki tribes continued to follow their traditional war plans of raid and retreat with goods and captives. Despite the French support they did not have the manpower or logistics to maintain occupation forces to keep the English settlers and soldiers from their territory.

The following year in May, two or three hundred Natives including the Kennebecs overwhelmed the Casco Bay fort's commander, Josiah Winslow, and soldiers who were traveling in longboats. Winslow and fifteen Englishmen and twenty-five Indians were killed.

Captain William Canady assumed command of the fort, which was promptly assaulted by the Wabanaki. They burned ships and dwellings. "While the vessels were burning they kept firing on all sides but we held them in Play and by heaving on water we prevent[ed] the fires doing any damage" to the fort, reported Canady. The war party retreated after several hours.

Massachusetts Lieutenant Governor William Dummer and the provincial legislature authorized the raising of 1,000 men at £60 and the bonus payments of £100 per scalp.

Governor Dummer decided to attack the Natives at Norridgewock where Father Sebastien Râle (Rale, Rasles) was encouraging resistance to the English. Dummer saw the priest as "a constant & Notorious Fomenter & Incendiary to the Indians to kill, burn, & destroy" English settlers, as he said in a later January 19, 1725, letter to Governor Vaudreuill.

Dummer believed that the destruction of the main Abenaki village on the Kennebec would end the raids and attacks on the settlers in western Maine.

To determine the truth of the events of the attack on Norridgewock is very difficult, given the multitude of differing reports. But I'll give it a try.

Fort Richmond on the Kennebec was the marshaling point for the attack on Norridgewock in August, 1724. Harmon and his brother-in-law, Jeremiah Moulton, led the English force. Moulton too had a personal stake in the attack. His parents had been killed and he had been captured during the Indian attack on York in 1692. He was later ransomed and returned to York. Moulton and Harmon became noted or infamous hunters of Abenakis.

Harmon and Moulton led 208 rangers up the Kennebec River in seventeen whaleboats toward Norridgewock, the main village of the Kennebec tribe. Two Mohawks, Old Christian, and Young Christian, and a Nauset, Jeremy Queach (killed in action) accompanied the Englishmen.

Moulton led the direct attack on the village, while Harmon's force surrounded the area through the corn fields.

The village was near the mouth of the Sandy River where the Wesserunset stream enters and the present town of Madison now stands.

Captain Joseph Heath had described the village in 1719. "Neridgwalk Fort, Built with Round Loggs nine foot long one end set into the Ground: is 160 foot square with 4 Gates but no Bastions; within it are Twenty six Houses built much after the English manner, the Streets regular, that from the west Gate to the East is 30 foot wide; their Church stands 4 perch without the East gate, and their men able to Bear Arms, are about Three Score."

On the way the English apparently killed Sachem Bomazeen's daughter to prevent her from warning the village.

According to an August 23 unfinished letter of Father Râle to Father de la Chassee, found by the English, the warriors had just come back and there were a number of visitors in the village. Nine Becancourian from Quebec had arrived. "Yesterday 12 or 15 Pannaouanskeians [Penobscots] four Hurons with One wounded arrived here almost Starved-Therefore They must be supplied tho the Corn is not ripe. They must take it as it is, for we are almost reduced to a Famine, Provisions being so scarce."

The Natives were preparing to "quit the Village for a fortnight to go five or six leagues up the River" after the corn was harvested.

According to Sachem Mogg, "they were preparing for and were to be joined by 200 men from Penobscut in a few Days," according to Captain Harmon.

Neither the peaceful nor the violent plan would come to fruition.

In his unfinished letter of August 23 Father Râle reported that "one of the bravest" Natives had warned of the coming attack. "My people are returned from their last Expedition, wherein one of their Bravest Champions was killed. Believing there were above two hundred English divided in three Parties or Bands to drive them out of their Camp, and Expecting a further number to enforce them in order to ruin all the Corn in the Fields without doubt.

But I said to them, how Could that be, Seeing we are daily surrounding and making Inroads upon them everywhere in the midst of their Land, and they not coming out of their Fort, which they have upon your own land. Besides in all the War, you have had with them, did you ever see them Come to Attack you in the Spring, Summer or in the fall; when they knew you were in your habitations. You know it, You say Yourselves that they never did, but when they knew you were not, but when you were in the Woods. For if they knew there were but fifteen or twelve Men in your dwellings they dare not Approach you with One hundred. We told you after the fall fight at Ke-ke-penagliesek that the English would come with the Nation of the Iroqouis to Revenge themselves. You opposed it and said they should not, and yet they did, you see now whether You are in the right."

And yet their leader was very wrong.

Moving overnight the English attacked during the day of August 23rd.

More than sixty Norridgewocks (Norridgewogs, Narantsouacks) were killed or wounded, including more than two dozen women and children. The Natives tried to escape in and across the river, but they were caught in the gunfire and savage attacks of the rangers. Quickly the river began to turn red from the blood of the Indians and rangers.

Richard Jacques [Jaques], Moulton s son-in-law, reportedly killed Father Râle. Moulton s old enemy Bomazeen fell with the priest. Chief Meesamouet of the Norridgewocks, and Chief Mogg Hegon [Mog], Wabanaki sachem of the Saco Tribe were also killed.

The dead and dying were scalped and soldiers later collected their bounties for twenty-eight scalps in Boston.

The village was burned and the corn crops destroyed. The survivors scattered-many went as far as St. Francois in Quebec.

The two Mitchell boys recently captured at Scarborough were rescued- providing proof, if proof was needed, of the guilt of the Norridgewock warriors.

The English force returned to Fort Richmond with twenty-eight or twenty-six scalps, four prisoners and three rescued English captives. The Norridgewock's main village was destroyed and the power of the tribe to defend its turf was shattered.

Some of the tribe s members returned to bury their dead and pick up the pieces of their village. Father Râle is now buried in St. Sebastien Cemetery in Madison.

Captain Harmon later gave this report to the Massachusetts Council on August 25th as quoted by Ekstorm. "There was not an Indian to be seen, being all in their wigwams. Our men were ordered to advance softly and to keep a profound silence. At length an Indian came out of one of the wigwams and discovered the English close upon him. He immediately gave the warwhoop and ran in for his gun.

"The warriors ran to meet the English, the rest fled to save their lives. Moulton, instead of suffering his men to fire at random through the wigwams, charged every man not to fire, upon pain of death, until the Indians discharged their guns. It happened as he expected; in their surprise they overshot the English, and not a man was hurt. The English then discharged in their turn, and made great slaughter, but every man still kept his rank. The Indians then fired a second volley, and immediately fled towards the river.

"They made the best of their way to the River, where they had about 40 Canoes; we followed them so close that they put off, without their Paddles, not having time to take them; we then presently beat them out of their Canoes, Killing the greatest part of them; the River being about 60 yards over and Shallow, our Men followed them over with such fury, that but one of their Canoes arrived upon the other side, but others Waded and Swam over, so that we judge about 50 Men, Women and Children got over.

"We then returned to the Town, where we found Monsieur Ralle the Jesuit, their chief Commander, in one of the Indians houses, who had been continuously firing upon a Party of our Men, that were still in the Town: the said Ralle having Wounded one of our people, Lieut. Jaques soon Stove open the door of said house, and found him loading his Gun, who upon Jaques's coming in, Declared Voluntarily, That he would give no quarter, nor take any; Jaques hearing that, and seeing him Loading, shot him thro' the head; the said Jesuit had with him an English Boy[Mitchell] about 14 Years of Age whom he had about Six Months in his Possession, which Boy, in the time of the Engagement, he spitefully shot thro' the Thigh, and stabbed him in the Body with a Sword, and so left him; but the Boy not being Dead, we took him with us, and thro' the Care and Skill of the Surgeon is like to recover."

Captain Harmon made this direct statement about the dead sachems: "The Chiefs that we know among the Dead, were the said Jesuit, Colonel Bomarzeen, Captain Mogg, Captain Job, Captain

Carabasset, Captain Wissememet, Bomarzeen's Son in law, and some others whose Names I cannot Remember."

Colonel Thomas Westbrook sent a letter to Dummer describing their success. "Capt. Harmon arrived this day with the Fryars and Twenty Six Scalps more from Norridgewock and brought Bomazees Squaw and three more Indian captives, retook three English boys, he informs a great number of Indians are coming on our frontier Sundry from Canada."

Westbrook continued: "Capt Harmon and the officers judge that by the modestes Computation besides the scalps and Captives they brought on, what they killed and drowned there could not be less than thirty or forty, God has been pleased to Crown your Honours unwearied Endeavors with success."

An account in the *Boston News-Letter* for August 28 adds a few more details. The next morning they left the village taking with them three barrels of gunpowder, some guns, blankets, knives, kettles, the church plate, four Indian captives and three English prisoners. "They marched early for Taconick, being in some pain for their men and whaleboats, but found all safe." Old Christian, a Mohawk whose brother had been killed by Mogg, went back to the village and "burnt all to Ashes, and coming up with us again, we Marched to Teuconick."

The French Governor Vaudreuil described the attack in a November 28, 1724, letter, which was translated in *New York Colonial Documents*. "The Village was surprised on the 23rd of August last. The English accompanied by some Indians, called La Porcelaine, arrived there under cover of the long grass and brushwood with which the environs were filled, and came on the cabins unawares.

"This village was without palisades and the Narantsousans [Nanrantsouack, Noridgewocks] considered themselves sufficiently secure there in consequence of the care they took to send out scouts.

"The Narantsousans then in the village numbered fifty warriors. Those who were not hit by the bullets which riddled the bark of the wigwams, having immediately rushed to arms, made a few moments resistance, crying to the women and children to fly to the river, which was yet open.

Father Râlle, the ancient missionary of the Abenakis, went out of his house on hearing the noise, but the moment he made his appearance the English fired a volley at him by which he was immediately killed.

"Those of the Indians who possessed not the courage to resist, fled towards the river as soon as they perceived that the Father was slain. The bravest of the warriors who had held out a long time against the English, seeing that they were on the point of being surrounded, flung themselves into the river like all the rest, and the English pursued them into the water's edge with their shots. Firing as they did, unimpeded, against a mass of frightened people who were crossing a river, some in canoes and some swimming, it is surprising that a single man should have escaped. They killed in this action only 7 men, 7 women, 14 children and wounded 14 persons very slightly. The mass of the village which escaped amounts to 150 persons, among whom there still remain 29 warriors."

In her historical novel, *In the Shadow of the Steel Cross,* Louise Hunt describes the climax of the attack on Norridgewock: "The Chiefs stood with their priest as the line of redcoat soldiers marched towards them with muskets directed to the front of the church. Within seconds the roar and blaze of gunfire echoed across the village. The brave men fell to the ground at the foot of the steel cross. Chiefs, Bomazeen, Mog, Carrabessett, Paugus, Wiwurna, Job and Wissememet fell by the body of Pere Râle. To the side lay the altar servers, Michael and Josh."

The same steel cross, according to Hunt, now stands in St. Anne's Catholic Church at Old Town, Maine.

The attack was described in some detail by Pierre Charlevoix, an eighteenth century French historian. "The 23rd of August, 1724, eleven hundred men, part English, part Indians, came up to Norridgewock. The thickets, with which the Indians village was surrounded, and the little care taken by the inhabitants to prevent a surprize, caused that the enemy were not discovered, until the very instant when they made a general discharge of their guns and their shot had penetrated all the Indian wigwams. There was not above fifty fighting men in the village. These took to their arms and ran out in confusion, not with any expectation of defending the place against the enemy who were already in possession, but to favor the escape of their wives, their old men and children, and to give them time to recover the other side of the river, of which the English had not then possessed themselves.

"The noise and tumult gave Father Ralle notice of the danger his converts were in. Not intimidated, he went to meet the enemy, in hopes to draw all their attention to himself and secure his flock at the peril of his own life. He was not disappointed. As soon as he appeared, the English set up a great shout, which was followed by a shower of shot, and he fell down dead near toa cross which he had erected in the midst of the village, seven Indians, who accompanied him to shelter him with their own bodies, falling dead round him. Thus died this kind shepherd, giving his life for his sheep, after a painful mission of thirty seven years. The Indians, who were all in the greatest consternation at his death, immediately took to flight, and crossed the river, some swimming and others fording. The enemy pursued them, until they had entered far into the woods where they again gathered together to the number of an hundred and fifty. Altho more than two thousand shot had been fired upon them, yet there were no more than thirty killed and fourteen wounded. The English, finding they had no body left to resist them, fell first to pillaging and then burning the wigwams. They spared the church, so long as was necessary for their shamefully profaning the sacred vessels and the adorable body of Jesus Christ, and then set fire to it. At length they withdrew, with so great precipitation that it was rather a flight, and they seemed to be struck with a perfect panick. The Indians immediately returned to their village, where they made it their first care to weep over the body of their holy missionary, whilst their women were looking out for herbs and plants for healing the wounded. They found him shot in a thousand places, scalped, his skull broke to pieces with the blows of hatchets, his mouth and eyes full of mud, the bones of his legs fractured and all his members mangled in an hundred different ways. Thus was a priest treated in his mission, at the foot of a cross, by those very men who have so strongly exaggerated the pretended inhumanity of our Indians, who have never made such carnage upon the dead bodies of their enemies. After his converts had raised up and oftentimes kissed the precious remains, so tenderly and so justly bellowed by them, they buried him in the same place where the evening before, he had celebrated the sacred mysteries, namely, where the altar stood, before the church was burnt."

Thomas Hutchinson summarized the victory by concluding: "The Norridgewock tribe never made any figure since this blow."

Samuel Penhallow called the attack "the greatest victory we have obtained in three or four last wars."

The attack was hailed in Boston as "a singular Work of God," by Rev. Benjamin Coleman.

"The wonderful Victory...over the bold and bloody Tribe at Norridgewock and their sudden Destruction that Memorable Day, was the singular Work of God."

Coleman continued to exult over Father Râle s death. "And he who was the Father of the War, the Ghostly Father of those perfidious Savages, like Balaam the Son of Beor, was slain among the enemy, after his vain Endeavours to Curse us."

Samuel Sewall, a noted Puritan diarist and judge, was only slightly less jubilant. "The Lord help us to rejoice with Trembling." But he noted in Boston there was "great Shouting and Trembling" in celebrating the victory.

James Franklin, Benjamin's older brother, printed a ballad, "The Rebels Reward," including a line about the death of Mogg's wife and two children "who were dispatch'd with speed."

Captain Harmon, on the recommendation of Colonel Westbrook, was promoted to lieutenant colonel and was given a £100 bonus for Father Râle's scalp.

Lieutenant Governor Dummer defended the killing of Father Râle in a long letter of January 19, 1724/25 to the French Governor Vaudreuil. "As to what you say relating to the Death of Mr. Ralle the Jesuit, which you set forth as so inhumane & barbarous, I readily acknowledge that he was slain amongst others of our Enemies at Norrigwalk, And if he had confin'd himself to the professed Duty of his Function vizt. To instruct the Indians on the Christian Religion, had kept himself within the bounds of the French Dominions & had not instigated the Indians to War & Rapine, there might then have been some ground for complaint. But when instead of preaching peace Love & Friendship agreeable to the Doctrines of the Christian Religion he has been a constant & notorious Fomenter & Incendiary as fragrantly appears by many original Letters & Manuscripts I have of his by me to the Indians to kill burn & destroy, and when in open violation of an Act of Parliament of Great Britain & the Lawes of this Province strictly forbidding Jesuits to reside or teach within British Dominions he has not only resided but also once & again appeared at the head of great Numbers of Indians in an hostile manner threatening & insulting as also publicly assaulting the Subjects of His British Majesty, I say, if after all, such an Incendiary has happened to be slain in the heat of Action among out open & declared Enemies, Surely none can be blamed therefor but himself, nor can any safeguard from you or any other Justify him in such proceedings."

On the other hand Catholic Bishop of Boston, Benedict Fenwick, erected a monument at Old Point in 1833 with this inscription: "Sebastian Ralle, a French Jesuit missionary, for many years the first evangelist among the Illinois and Hurons, and afterwards for thirty-four years a true apostle in the faith and love of Christ, among the Abenakies–unterrified by the danger, and often by his pure character, giving witness that he was prepared for death–this most excellent pastor, on the 23rd day of August, 1724, fell in this place, at the time of the destruction and slaughter of the town of Norridgewock, and the dangers to his church. To him, and to his children, dead in Christ, Benedict Fenwick, Bishop at Boston, has erected and dedicated this monument, this 23rd of August A.D. 1833."

Some of the Norridgewock tribe later returned to their old villages, but the tribe had been dealt a severe but not an existential blow.

The war was far from over.

Pequawket Indians raided Dunstable in 1724, and Captain John Lovewell led a force of rangers 130 miles up the Saco River.

Dummer ordered Westbrook in a September 28 letter to send more troops up the Kennebec "to surpirze the Enemy. It being probable the Corn left in those Parts or the Hunting may have drawn thither some of the Indians that escaped at Norridgewock."

By now the Eastern Native people were concentrated in two tribes, the Penobscot in far eastern Maine and the Norridgewock remnants along the Kennebec. The Mi kmaq and St. François Indians were in Canada, but still within reach of the Eastern settlements.

After the destruction of the Abenaki village at Norridgewock, English settlers began to move north along the river. Ultimately they would establish their own towns of Madison, Norridgewock and Anson in the same area.

On April 13, 1725, Indians were seen about Fort George and the Kennebec by Gyles. The next day he reported that a soldier had been captured by Natives but had escaped, who told him they had killed Moses Eaton, a Black man and another settler at Black Point. The man, James Cochron, escaped by killing and scalping his two guards. He reached Fort George with one scalp and Gyles then sent soldiers out to retrieve the lost scalp and furs. They returned on April 17 "with the author sculp, skins & in all to the value of 6 or 8 pounds."

Dummer ordered reinforcements for Gyles and directed him to send men up the rivers.

Colonel Westbrook reported to Dummer that "the Indians are down upon us in great number."

John Minot reported to Dummer in April 1725 that he had met with sachems from the Norridgewock and Penobscot tribes. They swore they wanted only peace and honest trading houses. They complained that the English shortchanged them and sold too much rum to the young men who then killed the cattle of Engliishmen. They complained that men like Chubb and Walton had killed Indians who were meeting them under peace treaties. Minot concluded that £500 of supplies would maintain peace with the Eastern Indians.

Within a month, on May 9 the Abenaki ambushed Captain John Lovewell near present day Fryeburg killing Lovewell and five other rangers. The English counted fifty-eight dead Pequawket warriors.

Lovewell's fight near Lovewell Pond was the last fight between the Wabanaki and the English settlers during Dummer's War.

By the end of the year both sides had had enough.

In December the commander of Fort George on Merrymeeting Bay was changed, John Gyles was replaced by William Woodside. The next year Woodside, the son of Rev. James Woodside, a former minister at Brunswick, was found guilty of cheating the Natives by underweighting their furs, watering down the rum and giving brass beads for gold beads. He was ordered to pay the Natives and promise not to do that again, but not removed from his post as commander of the fort. Apparently Woodside did not stop, because he was sued thirty years later for the same practices.

On the positive side William and his wife Ann Vincent boosted the local population with ten children.

The commonly called Treaty of Casco Bay of 1725 was first agreed to in Boston in December 1725, then at Annapolis Royall on June 4, 1726;and then at Falmouth in Casco Bay in July 1727.

Loron and Meganumbe, representing the Maliseet, Mi'kmaq, Penobscot and Norridgewock (Kennebec) tribes, negotiated the

Treaty of 1725 at Boston on December 15-16, 1725, with Lt. Governor Dummer. Arexies, Francois Xavier and Lignum joined Loron and Meganumbe in signing the treaty. According to John Penhallow's diary, the participants spoke in a mixture of French, English and Abenaki and "The Gent could not interpret it."

The treaty was then brought to Annapolis Royall, where it was read by interpreters, John Gyles, Samuel Jordan and Joseph Bane and signed by leaders of the Cape Sable and St. John tribes on June 4, 1726.

Still the struggle went on. According to Gyles, Louis, a Penobscot leader, told him the French Governor, Marquis de Beauharnois, had directed the Abenaki "to set a mark in the Kenebeck River above taconack, two men shaking hands and if Like to War, then to have a hatchek in Each hand, for those that Pass & Repass to View and be on their Guard, for several ar Expected with their families in the Spring to Settle aGain at Narrangawawock &c."

Gyles added that "This Day (March 3, 1727) Moxses, The Chief of Narrangawock Received his Lettars & Present," from Governor Dummer, "And he desiars me to acquaint, that he heartily salutes your honour, and Councell with his Cap on the Ground and is thankful for his Present and Lettar and Rejioyces to see your well wishing to Loue, & welfare of our Peoplle, on our land, he Rackens him sefl weak, tho as God would inable him, they shall not be wanting on their part, for the Same, hoping this summer after his tribe Coms over and settled—your honour will see their resolve for Love & Unity."

The treaty was then brought on to Falmouth on July 27, 1727, where leaders of the Norridgewock, Wawenock, Penobscot and Anasagunticook (Androscoggin) signed the same treaty.

After blaming the Abenaki tribes for the hostilities, basically both sides agreed that the English would live in permanent settlements based on agriculture, fishing, industry and lumbering. The Natives "shall not be molested in their persons, Hunting, Fishing and Planting Ground nor in any other Lawful Occasions by his Majesty's Subjects or their dependents."

Both sides promised not to take private revenge, but to seek redress within the English government and courts.

Natives "will cease and forbear all Acts of Hostility, Injuries and Discord towards all subjects of the Crown of Great Britain."

"All Captives taken in this present War...be restored without any Ransom or payment," said the treaty.

"That his Majesties Subjects the English shall be made peaceable and Quietly enter upon, Improve & forever enjoy all & singular rights of land and former Settlements, Properties & possessions with the Eastern Parts" of Massachusetts.

Penobscot, Norridgewock and other tribes shall have "their lands, liberties & properties not by them Conveyed or sold to or possess'd by any of the English."

The Indians have "also the Privilege of Fishing, Hunting & fowling as formerly."

Massachusetts was given the sole right to manage all trade and commerce with the tribes. As a result they enlarged the truck-houses at Richmond and St. Georges.

The Native signatories promise that all the tribes within the French territory "shall cease and desist from acts of hostility."

The Penobscot tribes promised to join in "reducing" hostile Indians "to reason."

They agreed that this treaty would also apply to all tribes within the province of New Hampshire.

The tribal leaders were to meet at Falmouth in Casco Bay in May 1726 to ratify this treaty.

The various tribal leaders met in Falmouth in 1727 and in Annapolis Royall in 1726.

Unfortunately, neither side accepted the concessions made to the other. English settlers returned in overwhelming numbers without regard to prior land ownership and the increase in settlers disrupted the Natives' abilities to maintain their hunter/gatherer lifestyle. The destruction of fur bearing animals by the Natives and the English settlers prohibited the Indians from procuring the means to buy supplies, guns and clothing from the English truck houses.

By 1725 the English population of Massachusetts including Maine is estimated to have been well over one hundred thousand compared to the estimate of the Indian population provided by John Gyles.

These numbers made resistance by Natives futile and the end of their way of life certain..

A year after the 1725 treaty ending Dummer's War, Captain Gyles reported a drastic decline in the number of male Indigenous People sixteen or older in the Dawnland. According to Gyles' memorandum prepared for Governor Dummer on November 24, 1726, there were 389 men among the various tribes. Despite the sacking of Norridgewock, Gyles reported thirty under Chief "Rewenadondo" and forty with Chief "Toxus." The Androscoggin under Chief "John Hegon" could muster only ten or five from nearly one hundred warriors. Chiefs "Ersegontegog" and "Mamereguenet" at St. François, which included many refugees from the Kennebec, numbered twenty. The Maliseets (his former masters) on the St. John River had one hundred men and the Penobscots had one hundred and thirty men, according to Gyles.

Gyles reported that the Pigwacket warriors were reduced from one hundred to twenty-four, the Saco men from fifty to four.

The accuracy of Gyles' report can not be confirmed, but it is clear that the Eastern Abenaki no longer had the manpower to prevent the flood of English settlers, fishermen and lumbermen from overwashing the Native lands and people.

After signing the 1725 treaty, Massachusetts authorized the spending of £4000 to reinforce forts and the promised truck houses for the Abenaki at Richmond on the Kennebec River, Union Falls on the Saco River and St. Georges on the St. Georges River as the most eastern outpost.

Massachusetts also attempted to settle a line of new towns in the Eastern District that would serve as buffers for the more populous coastal towns. In addition to defense, the towns would protect "His Majesty's Woods fir for the Masting the Royal Navy" and provide "room for many of the Inhabitants of this Province made for their Comfortable Subsistence."

One group of Wabankis, led by Sabatis, asked the government in 1727 to provide a truck house at Merrymeeting Bay, because "in cold winters and deep snows, my men [are] unable to go to Fort Richmond, sometimes suffer." But Richmond on the Kennebec remained the truck house for the Abenaki on the Kennebec.

The chiefs (Wywroney, Ommoway and Pere Sunc) of the remaining Norridgewock, Wawenock and St. François tribes petitioned Governor Dummer in June, 1727, asking for supplies and "Victuals." They said they were greatly weakened by the last war and needed support from the English, which was no doubt good news to the English. But wasn t it counterproductive for the English to supply the tribes that have been attacking them. Especially as Gyles discussed giving the Indians guns and ammunition as gifts.

With the fur trade nearly finished and the captive ransom/trade in serious decline, the Abenaki had to turn to the English for support, even subsistence. Dependence not independence became the feature of tribal life in the Dawnland.

Nevertheless, Dummer promised in a June 17 letter to meet them at Fort Richmond and "to establish a happy and lasting Friendship" like the one settled with the Penobscots.

The Chiefs responded in a letter to Dummer thanking Dummer, and in the mind of Gyles, "it was worthy of your honours perusing."

At the same time wealthy and influential men in Boston began to see vast profits in the sale of land and the harvesting of timber.

One group resurrected the old Pejepscot Patent of 1632 controlling vast quantities of land along the Kennebec and Androscoggin rivers.They had already boosted support for settlers in Brunswick, Topsham and north along the Kennebec.

Further eastward Samuel Waldo had consolidated ownership of the Muscongus Patent claiming a huge stretch of land between the Muscongus and Penobscot rivers. Waldo immediately began promoting his holdings in the German states and brought them to Broad Bay centered around the area that became Waldoborough and Bremen.

Many of those Germans from the Palatines, Wurttemberger and Switzerland later served with Waldo in the 1745 capture of Louisbourg resulting in another large grant of land to Waldo which was contiguous and sometimes overlapped the Muscongus Patent.

All these actions put additional pressure on the Native tribes.

In November 1730 Governor Jonathan Belcher sent Lieutenant Governor William Tailer and several other officials on a tour of the forts and truck houses in the Eastern District. Benjamin Larabee sent the governor a detailed account of their trip beginning with Fort Richmond on November 3. After meeting with the fort's commander, Captain Joseph Heath, they told "some Indians who we discovered near the Fort" that we intended to come ashore.

"Immediately after our landing an Indian Man commonly called Capt John of the Norridgewock with about thirteen men & the like number of Women & Children came up to the Fort." They told them they would give them presents with a message tomorrow. The Indians gave them a "small pack of River Skins" but "of little value."

The next day Tailer gave them blankets and other presents, saying "This is given you in Consideration of your past good Demeanour towards his Majesties good Subjects. He told them they must adhere to the Treaty of 1726.

That afternoon "we took a View of the House Built for the reception of the Indians which stands about half a mile from Fort Richmond and is very Conveniently situated for that end."

On November 5 they went down river to Fort George which they found "out of repair" and then down east to Fort St. Georges.

Massachusetts officials continued to support (bribe) Indians at the forts. For example, Toxus and other Norridgewock tribal members were provided "provision & drink" at Fort Richmond" on June 11, 1729. The commander at Fort Richmond reported on April 30, 1730, spending £4.3.5 over an eighteen month period for "an Indian" who "Secretly informes me of the Counsels & Determinations of the French and Indians from time to time."

After Dummer's War the Norridgewocks and Penobscots were sharply divided between those who wanted to live in peace with the English (labeled conciliators by David L. Ghere) and those who wanted continued hostilities or "malcontents". Over the next decades the hostiles fought back but increasingly migrated to Canada. The conciliators tried to remain in the Dawnland villages, but were often swept up in the violence by the English on the one hand trying to destroy the Indians and their fellow tribesmen who worked to involve them in their attacks on the English.

Despite the good intentions of the Massachusetts government to establish fair practices at the truck houses, there were constant complaints. The prices were too high. The goods were shoddy. The furs were inferior. The prices for furs were too low.

Truck-masters were paid £100 a year. Thinking this insufficient, Joseph Heath of Richmond successfully petitioned the province to allow truck-masters a ten percent commission on goods sold to cover losses on corn, molasses, sugar, rum, tobacco and other perishables.

By the late 1730's the fort and truck house at Richmond had become more of a "hub of frontier social and economic interaction" than a trading house for the Norridgewock. A surviving ledger of John Minot, truckmaster at Richmond, for 1737-1742, reveals that only three Natives (Quenois, Pramegen, and Packamumbanet) traded there and they were elderly employees of the truck house. On two occasions in 1738 and 1739 Minot gave £60 in presents from the governor to the Norridgewock tribe.

In contrast forty-eight white men and two white women had accounts there.

The records show a busy frontier settlement with carpenters, cobblers, farmers, millers and lumbermen.

But still there were conflicts between the English and Natives. On October 28, 1740 there was a conference at Fort Richmond over the killing of cattle and horses by Indians. Captain Joseph Beane, the interpreter, demanded that the Indians pay £18 for "Macob's ox," £6 for "Salley's steer" and £20 for "Patrick Drummond's horse." Whether the payments were made is not known, but these issues were being discussed in subsequent "conferences" between government officials and Native sachems.

During this period of peace the English economy boomed with expanding shipbuilding and lumbering. Immigrants from non-English speaking countries were encouraged by the great proprietors, such as Samuel Waldo, but also by the Massachusetts government. Meanwhile, the fur trade declined and many Natives moved to Canada.

On the eve of the renewal of warfare which became known as King George's War, the Penobscot Chief Loron, speaking for "the Rest" of the Penobscots and Kennebecs, sent a letter on February 11, 1742, to Massachusetts Governor William Shirley, complaining of their treatment by the traders at the truck house and also describing one of the many minor incidents of conflict between the English and the Natives that made peace difficult to maintain. Although the letter was written by Jabez Bradbury, an interpreter and former truck-master at Fort Richmond, it no doubt contains the thoughts and emotions of Loron. The claim that no one at Fort St. Georges spoke the Abenaki language highlights the difficulties the Natives and English had in communicating. The letter also reveals how dependent the Wabanakis had become on the English to supply even basic foods and supplies.

"Loron speaks in the name of the Rest. This Winter when our two men went to Boston and came back again they told us what you said to them which is all one as if we had recd a Letter.

You know there is no body understands Indian at [Fort St.] Georges and that was the reason we could not send an answer to what you sent us—and now we come to Richmond where our language is understood.

"Our hearts are towards you ever since you have bin in Government. The men that came from Boston told us you designed to see us at Georges. We should all be much Rejoyc'd to see you there for we cannot conveniently meet you farther westward.

"We much like your promise to comply with Governor Dummers agreement with us. One thing we dont like (which we agreed upon with Govr Dummer) we apprehend is not complyed with which was that if any goods rise our furrs were to Rise with them.

"We solemnly agreed with Govr Dummer that we should have our furrs at Georges Truckhouse as they are sold for at Boston. Your Excely may please to inquire of Governor Dummer the Treasurer and other Mechts who by furs whether we have justice done us on this head.

The Truckmaster here gives us [for beavers] 8/ for Saples [sables] 16/ for Spring bever 18/ for Otter 20/ for Cats? We now are kept much in the dark as to our trade. The man that manages it understands very little as to our language or trade his being a Minister we a little wonder at his coming to trade here.

"It was also agreed at Casco that we Should allwayes have a full Supply of Provisions and other things we need. Now we want all sorts of Provisions and many other nessasryes and have a long time bin without them in the middle of Winter the most necessary time we could want them in.

"We should be glad there is a man at Georges that understood trading with us and the Language. [John Dennis was the Truckmaster] Our men mentioned Jabez Bradbury [later commander at Fort St. Georges] unto your Excellency we like him well.

"For want of Provisions and through a mistake we have kild three horses at Sacadahock on Small Point side. We understood they were wild and free for any body accordingly we dryd the flesh openly. Two Days after we kild them six men came to us with their guns cockt demanding Satisfaction. upon their appearing in such a hostile manner we flew to our guns one of our men being wise told us we had better surrender our armes then to begin a quarrel which might be attended with such ill consiquences and not well understanding what these men said to us we delivered them four guns and two hatchets as a pledge for pay for the horses they insisting (as we understood them) to take them by violence if we did not resign them.

"We promise pay for the horses in the Spring upon the delivery of our guns.

"We are all in good health & give our love and Service to your Excely."

Strange that Loron should complain that no one at Fort St. Georges spoke or understood the Abenaki language, because Captain Gyles, the commander of the fort since 1728 had been an interpreter since 1701. On the other hand, Loron become happy when Jabez Bradbury, the interpreter at Fort Richmond, became the commander of Fort St. Georges later in 1742.

Although the list was for 1703, the Massachusetts Council approved list of goods supplied to the Natives and the prices they were to receive for their furs at Kennebec and other truck houses is illustrative. Three beaver skins would get you one yard of broadcloth. But most items were valued against one beaver skin "in season:" 1 ½ yard of gingham; 5 pecks of corn; 5 pecks of Indian meal; 4 pecks of peas; 2 pounds of powder; 2 pounds of shot; 6 fathom of tobacco; 6 knives; 1 hat; 1 shirt; 2 kettles; 2 small axes; 1 sword blade; and 3 dozen small hooks. No guns were listed for sale-but they were sold unofficially.

Furs listed as equivalent to one beaver in season: 1 otter; 1 bear skin; 2 foxes; 2 woodchucks; 4 martins; 8 minks; 4 raccoons; 4 seals; and five pounds of feathers. One moose skin was equal to two beaver skins. No deer skins were listed.

These prices would be a key subject of another conference of Indians and Governor Shirley in 1742.

It is a credit to the Natives for their persistence in speaking their own languages, and seemingly not understanding English despite more than a century of interaction. On the other hand few Englishmen who regularly interacted with the Indians bothered to learn the Abenaki language. Also this cultural persistence is one interpretation of the Indigenous people's inability to sign their names in English, but most used symbols and a mark (usually an X) for their signatures even on formal documents like treaties and deeds.

In response to Loron s letter, Governor William Shirley traveled to Fort St. Georges in early August 1742. There he met with thirty-five leaders of the various Wabanaki tribes: Penobscot, Norridgewock, Pigwacket (Saco, Amiscoggin), St. Johns (Maliseets) and St. François. After a sumptuous dinner the English and thirty-five Native representatives settled down to negotiations. Shirley acknowledged the complaints in Loron s letter. Loron of the Penobscot Tribe and Moxus,, sachem of the Norridgewock tribe, spoke for all the sachems.

Moxus told the governor he is "now heartily glad at the sight of the Governor."

Loron, backed by Moxus, argued that trade is the "chief Band of our Peace and Friendship."

The French gave them free powder and shot, according to Loron. A fact, Governor Shirley would later deflect by saying the English gave them many presents.

The sachems also asserted that the English had promised lower prices for goods than the French charged, but they hadn't delivered.

Moxus was more specific. "The Gentleman that was ordered to Richmond to trade is gone from thence; not but we lik'd Capt Minot very well at Richmond; and the Gun Smith that is there we like very well, Mr. Wood. We should be glad he would be our Truck Master. The Reason of my mentioning him is because the Penobscot tribe had mentioned Jabez Bradbury before for this truck-house, who would have been agreeable to us."

Moxus also stated he agreed with Loron on the trade issues.

Governor Shirley said they would adhere to the Dummer Treaty and that their goods are cheaper than the French. He argued that the prices are higher since 1727, but so are prices for beaver pelts of less quality. . .

He gave several examples: beaver was 9s per pound and is now 16s per pound; Stroud blankets were 30s and now 50s; corn was 7s per bushel and now 10s; powder was 4s per pound and now 7s; shot was 10d per pound and now 19d.

Shirley's conclusion was that poorer beaver pelts now buy more goods. He asserted the government loses money on the sale of goods. He did agree that the Truck Masters would be required to "give a Bill of Parcels of the quantity and price of Beaver" and that the prices should be posted. The governor promised the same prices as "Beaver & other Skins as they fetch in Boston."

Loron and Moxus complained they "can't understand Cyphering" so to give money for pelts "as we dont understand we are cheated."

Loron insisted they had been promised free powder and shot. "It was told to us so then [ie 1727]."

Loron and Moxus complained that they get lower prices for sable and bear skins, which are now scarce. Shirley replied that the pelts sell for less in Boston.

Both sides agreed that they need "suitable and honest" men at the truck houses.

The Sachems and Governor then turned to the issue of restrictions on the Englishmen's intrusions into the interior beyond the tidal water, or as Loron said "where the Fresh water runs."

The Indians asserted that the "young Englishmen" were not supposed to go into the woods to hunt as they "will destroy our Livelihood."

Loron stated: "The English till the ground, and have other Ways to support themselves."

Shirley asserted they were following Dummer's Treaty and any disputes should be settled in English courts.

Loron reminded the governor that they should stick to the land agreement and "not to go a Foot over the Line agreed to."

Shirley asserted that Madockawando had deeded the English the land around the St. Georges River for "a hatt full of Pieces of eight and Sundry Blankets."

Loron replied that Madockawando "never was a Proprietor of Land here, and we have heard so often about him. We don't desire any more."

Shirley insisted the English had purchased the land and any disputes would be settled in English courts. He also promised that conforming to the 1727 treaty they would "not about settling any Lands on the East side of the River [St.Georges].

A promise already broken by the Samuel Waldo settlers.

Loron claimed that they had not let the French settle on their rivers, but "we have shown more regard to the English, than any other white People, being desirous to live in Friendship with them."

Shirley promised the English would not settle more than they have a right to and will not "crowd your settlements"

Both sides then turned to specific incidents of Natives killing horses and cattle and Englishmen killing Natives' dogs.

Shirley insisted that the Indians must pay for damages to horses, hogs, and cattle killed by them.

Loron responded that perhaps the Indians did not kill them. "It may be vermin have killed them."

Bears or wolves might be responsible, he argued.

Shirley argued that there were many cases with witnesses.

They both turned to the incident of the three horses. Loron claimed the case was closed because the English had confiscated the Natives' guns and not returned them.

Moxus argued that "the Cattle killed by Ackumbuett's son and my son" was because "they were in Liquor and hardly knew what they did; when I came to know I paid 25s for them."

Shirley retorted that money was for another horse and steer. To which Moxus admitted: "It is true. I am mistaken. "

Shirley asserted that they must pay for the depredations and that they "ought to do all you can to restrain your Young men."

Loron replied sarcastically: "We are old men, and cant have Eyes every where."

Shirley then gave an ox and liquor for a goodbye dinner.

Loron finished for the tribes: "We harbour no Evil in our Breasts but are sincere and upright in what we say; and could your Excellency look into our Hearts, you would not be able to find any corrupt Nature in us."

Both sides promised peace and friendship.

And so back to business.

When war was renewed between France and England in the War of Austrian Succession in Europe in 1740 there was little immediate effect in America. The French in Canada tried their best to entice the Eastern Indians into attacking the English. In March 1744, the French Governor Beauharnois lured many of the Norridgewocks and Penobscots to Quebec with offers of presents and supplies if they would help attack the English. King George's War, as it was known in New England, got off to a slow start in the northeast, because the Abenaki were reluctant to begin another war. A war they sensed based on past events, that they could not win.

But professional Indian hunters almost forced the Penobscots into the war, when they attacked a Penobscot village in October 1744 killing one warrior and wounding several other Indians.

The Massachusetts government paid the widow for her loss, and asked the Norridgewocks and Penobscots to join in an alliance against the French. They refused.

Meanwhile the New England provinces led by Massachusetts, planned to rid themselves of French and Indian attacks by destroying the French fortress of Louisbourg on Cape Breton Island. In the spring of 1745 with help from the British navy a large force of New England militia, led by men like Colonel Samuel Waldo, besieged the fortress which was defended by French soldiers, militia and Mi'kmaq warriors. The fort fell in June 1745 making instant heroes of the military leaders. More importantly for the English in the Dawnland, it kept most of the Mi'kmaqs in Acadia.

Also important for the settlement of Maine was a grant of twenty-nine square miles of land between the St. Georges and Penobscot Rivers to Samuel Waldo for his military service. Added to Waldo's control of the old Muscongus Patent it gave Waldo and his partners "ownership" of nearly one million acres, most of which was to have been reserved to the Penobscots for hunting grounds. Waldo's aggressive settlement efforts since the seventeen thirties added to the pressure on the conciliatory branch of the Penobscots.

Still there were enough Penobscots, Mi'kmaqs and Frenchmen to attack Fort St. George's where the garrison had recently been expanded to one hundred men. On July 19, 1745, seventy Natives attacked the fort and neighboring settlement, according to Governor Shirley's July 22, letter. "On Saturday evening last I received an account from Capt. Bradbury of a grat number of Indians attacking the Fort at St. Georges River, burning several houses on that river killing a great number of cattle, and killing or taking one of the inhabitants."

Bradbury reported that almost seventy Indians attacked, killed fifty or sixty head of cattle, besides hogs and horses, and killed or captured one man. Even though they set fire to one of the block houses, they were repulsed.

Bradbury demanded that the Penobscots "give up" the warriors who had participated. They refused.

When the Penobscots remained in the area and even came to the fort to trade in September, Bradbury took matters into his own hands. He led an attack on the Indian encampment on Mill River, killing two–"Col. Morris," and "Capt. Sam," "Col. Job" was captured and one Indian escaped.

According to Governor Shirley's December 25, 1745, report to the General Court: "about 14 days since, sundry persons came up from St.George's with the scalps of two Penobscot Indians which they had killed, and one of that tribe they had taken captive, with an expectation to receive the bounty for them." The governor declined to pay it, because of the belief that these were peaceful Abenakis. Job later died in prison, and his wife was given a blanket as recompense.

At the same time Norridgewock and Penobscot warriors attacked Pemaquid. Governor Shirley in a July 25 report to the General Court described the attack ."I have also to inform you, that I received yesterday an Express from Capt. Savage, at his Majesty's Fort Frederic, advising me , that on the 19th Instant, a party of Indians had seized a woman [Mrs. McFarland] within Three hundred yards of the Fort, but that she breaking from them had, under cover of the Fire from the Fort, escaped into it with receiving only one Wound in her shoulder with a Musquet Ball; and that he was in hourly Expectation of having the Fort itself attacked by a large Party of the Enemy."

On the Kennebec the residents of Bath sent Edward Hutchinson to ask the General Court to exempt the town from taxes during the war. While at the same time in 1745 and 1746 they asked the General Court to provide funds for additional troops and guards for the lumbering crews. They also asked for "supplies of men to cover us."

On August 23 Massachusetts declared war on the Eastern Abenaki in Maine.

As a result, over the next two years nearly 600 Penobscots and Norridgewocks left their villages on the Kennebec and Penobscot rivers for Canada: Norridgewocks at Becancour and Penobscots at Pannaouemske.

But still the fighting went on with the Natives raiding the eastern settlements.

On May 22, 1746, eight Penobscots ambushed a party of men working in the woods along the Kennebec. Eliakim Hunt was killed and Timothy Cushing was taken prisoner. Four other English men were wounded. Two Indians were killed and scalped by the Englishmen in this brief engagement.

That same month Abenakis raided the English settlement at Broad Bay [Bremen]. The buildings were all destroyed but the inhabitants all escaped to Fort Frederic.

At about the same time, Natives attacked the outlying farm of John McFarland. Several in the family were wounded and the buildings destroyed.

The provincial sloops constantly ranged along the coast sailing up the Kennebec and St. Georges Rivers providing protection from raids from the ocean and bringing needed supplies to the forts.

These damaging raids continued into 1747.

Warriors from the Norridgewock and Penobscot tribes infested the woods around the settlements on the Kennebec, St. Georges and Pemaquid rivers.

The garrison at Fort Richmond became restless, and Governor Shirley sent Colonel Jonathan Moulton to quell "a discontented & Muntinous Disposition at Richmond" by replacing the men in the garrison.

A force of French and Indians invested Fort St. Georges in September, 1747. Even trying to tunnel under the fort from the river bank. The attack failed, but one soldier and a settler, David Creighton, were killed and scalped not far from the fort.

Closer to home Norridgewocks and other Wabanakis killed two women, Jane and Elizabeth Lermond in Walpole on April 27. Around the same time fifteen English settlers, including a woman and six children, were killed or captured on the west bank of the Damariscotta River in what is now Newcastle.

More than one hundred French and Indians surrounded Fort Frederic on May 26, but they failed to overcome the stone walls of the fort. Nevertheless, five men were killed: John and Joseph Cox, Vincent, Smith and Weston. Three others were taken prisoner.

In September the Indians returned to Pemaquid, ambushing several people outside the fort. Three men were killed and two were wounded, and presumed captured. Around this time the same Indians caught George and Walter McFarland working on John's

Island. George was killed and Walter captured by the Penobscots, with whom he remained for two years before being exchanged in Falmouth.

In 1748, the year that would bring another peace treaty, Norridgewocks raided around Brunswick and North Yarmouth.

The Treaty of Aix-la-Chapelle in 1748 restored peace, but also returned the Fortress of Louisbourg to the French. Not a popular outcome with the English settlers in the Dawnland.

Most of the Eastern Abenakis who had retreated to Canada slowly began to return to their villages. In their absence the English settlers had expanded even further up the rivers and into the interior. There was little the Wabanaki tribes could do.

With a shaky peace in place in 1749, the garrisons were reduced to twenty-four at Fort Richmond, forty-five at Fort St. Georges, and twenty-four at Pemaquid. The local militias and volunteer Indian hunters also ranged through the woods scouting for Indians.

The most important 1749 event for the settlers and Natives on the Kennebec River was the first meeting of the Kennebeck Proprietors. Based on the Plymouth Patent of 1629 granted by the Council of New England and enlarged in 1630 the proprietors claimed all land within ten miles of the Kennebec River. The Kennebeck Company did not care about Indian deeds. Thereby destroying any leverage the Wabanaki had left, while at the same time overturning the land claims of settlers based on rival companies and/or Indian deeds. With the wealth and power of its members, and the political support of Governor Shirley, a newly gifted member, there would now be a new boss along the Kennebec. The post-1727 status quo on the Kennebec, according to Ian Saxine, would soon be destroyed.

The sachems of the Penobscot and Norridgewock tribes traveled to Boston to request another peace conference, which was set for September 1749 in Falmouth.

Nineteen Indians from the Norridgewock, Penobscot, St. François and Anasagunticook tribes met five commissioners from Massachusetts. Toxus, Eneas, Magawombee, Sacarry Harry,

Sooseph, Naktoonos, Nesquambuit and Peerez attended from the Norridgewock.They reaffirmed the treaty ending Dummer s war and promised mutual and cordial friendship.

Toxus summed up the Natives agreement: "We have agreed to follow the Path of Governor Dummer's treaty; We desire to turn all the Blood upon the Ground, under it; and that all may be forgotten." Toxus might as well have desired the Kennebec River to flow into Canada instead of Merrymeeting Bay and the Atlantic Ocean.

To further limit the effects of the conference, only the conciliatory Natives attended the treaty conference, while the hostile Norridgewocks and Penobscots remained in Canada.

Moreover, a Penobscot chief, Loron, had lost a son in battle in 1747, and swore revenge whenever the opportunity arose. At the same time, English settlers' anger was stoked, not only by Indian attacks, but by the attempts of agents of the Kennebeck/Pejebscot proprietors to collect money for land sales and to dispossess squatters from company land.

Several Norridgewocks and Penobscots became unfortunate victims of English sailors on their way home from the peace conference. Sacarry Harry, a Norridgewock, and three others stopped to fish in the Sheepscot River at present day Wiscasset.

Visiting sailors attacked the small band of Native families fishing and hunting on December 2, 1749. Norridgewock sachem, Saccary Harry, was killed. Two others were wounded, Job, a Norridgewock, and Andrew, from St. François, but they escaped.

Two of the men's wives persuaded the local magistrates to investigate the crime. Six sailors were arrested and one, Obadiah Albee, escaped on a schooner bound for Marblehead.

Four of those arrested were immediately released, but Samuel Ball and Benjamin Ledite were sent to Falmouth for trial. Ball and Ledite were freed by a mob in Falmouth but later recaptured.

The Reverend Thomas Smith noted in his diary for January 11, 1750: "There has been a great uproar about the men that killed the Indian at Witchcassit, they having been rescued by some of our people from the officers, and today after surrendering themselves to Capt. Bean at the truck-house, were carried to York."

Anger swept through the local tribe, but they were persuaded to await the outcome of the English trial.

Accordingly they were to be put on trial for murder.

Albee was arrested in Marblehead and returned to York County for trial in June 1750.

He was actually tried in York County Superior Court, but was found innocent much to the anger of the Abenakis.

Ball escaped and was never tried. Ledite was found guilty of assault on Job and Andrew and sentenced to be whipped.

In an effort to assuage the Norridgewocks, the government gave the widow £19.10.6, including 34 biscuits, 6 ginger cakes, 2 quarts of rum, 2 blankets, 7 pounds of pork, 3 quarts of molasses, 2 yards of flannel, and 1 hatchet.

The hostile Abenaki demanded revenge, but most of the conciliatory villagers on the Kennebec refused to go to war. The French Intendant Bigot complained that the "conciliatory factions"

were "so connected with the English, they did not wish to insist on Justice."

In 1750 a joint committee of the Massachusetts legislature led by William Pepperrell traveled to Fort Richmond to negotiate a new treaty with the Norridgewock tribe. Four of the Kennebeck Proprietors, James Bowdoin, William Brattle, Jacob Wendell and Samuel Godwin, were representatives from Massachusetts. William Skinner was a member of the neighboring Pejepscot Company. All had a vested interest in the treaty, because they were already selling land and settling colonists along the Kennebec River.

The result was a reaffirmation of the Treaty of Falmouth of 1749, but it sufficed to maintain relative peace on the Kennebec for just a year. In 1749 both sides had agreed to return captives; Natives agreed to live in "amity with all the English; Indians to end alliance with France; English colonists can safely occupy all their "former settlements in the Eastern Parts"; Massachusetts to regulate all trade;

and if there are any hostile Indians the signatories will "reduce" any Indians committing hostile acts "to reason."

Within a year the Abenakis from Norridgewock and St. François attacked the houses and families of James Whidden and Lazarus Noble on Swan Island in the Kennebec River. Whidden told the Massachusetts government: "That in the late Excursion of the Indians on the Eighth day of September last [1750], early in the morning his House was surrounded with a Party of Indians to the number of Twenty or thereabouts, who in a hostile manner did enter into his House, destroying and plundering all his Furniture and carried away all they could of any Value; Your Memorialist with his wife saved themselves by getting down the Cellar which they had but time to do without putting on their Cloaths to cover their Nakedness."

Whidden's two sons, his daughter, his son-in-law Noble, seven grandchildren and two servants [Jabez Chubb and Hannah Holmes] were all taken captive to Canada.

Whidden warned the fort, but the Abenakis laid siege to the fort for three hours, while they killed the settlers' cattle. They also burned the house of Widow Weymouth and captured Philip Jenkins, who had left the fort. There was little the garrison of seven soldiers could do.

Symbolically, Samuel Goodwin and his party of eight men were surveying the land for the Kennebeck Proprietors and they retreated to the fort.

That same day, September 8, the Abenaki warriors threatened Fort Richmond, but only managed to capture Phillip Jenkins, who had gone out of the fort early in the morning. In Canada he was bought by S. Bazin for 250 livres, but soon died at a Quebec hospital on October 28, 1750.

At Brunswick John Martin (Marten) was captured while "at Labour in his own fields", and redeemed himself from Sieur Joseph Cadut (Cadet) with a note for 260 livres and "obtained permission of the Governor General to return to New England." The first to return, Martin reached Boston on January 25, 1751. He later returned to Brunswick.

The Abenaki warriors then moved on to Wiscasset and Sheepscot. The Norridgewocks told the English that they had not participated but it was Abenakis from Canada. Lieutenant Governor Spencer Phips had warned Ezekiel Cushing on September 14 not to attack the Norridgewocks on the Kennebec because they had warned the English of the "designs of the Arresagunticooks against us" and so "it is probable that they are desirous of remaining in peace with us."

In an October 6, 1750, letter William Lithgow told Lieutenant Governor Phips that "two of the Narrigewack Tribe" had reported the Indians had been at Norridgewock but had gone straight to Canada with their captives.

The Natives, numbering about sixty, captured John Martin at Brunswick, William Ross and son John at Sheepscot (Newcastle) and burned the garrison house. Contemporaries interpreted this raid as revenge for the unpunished killing of the Indians at Wiscasset.

William Ross' wife petitioned the General Court for assistance in April 16, 1751, because their house had been burned and her husband, "a lame man" was a captive in Canada and she had three small children to support. The General Court refused to assist her; they did not want to "give Encouragement to the Indians & french to go on in the Same methods." In other words they did not want to continue the process of capture, sale and ransom of English settlers.

Mrs. Ross returned to her father's garrison house in Brunswick. They were redeemed through Crown Point, and returned to Sheepscot.

Two days later, Reverend Smith of Falmouth reported: "We hear that on Saturday all Kennebec was in a blaze firing guns."

Lieutenant Bradbury at Fort St. Georges later reported that Penobscots told him the Swan Island raid was in revenge of Wiscasset and they "will hunt us no more." Returning captive Martin, stated the attack was "because the English made war first by firing on their men and killing one and wounding one."

Spencer Phips accused Governor LaJonquière in an October 1750 letter of urging the Natives to attack the English, resulting in capturing twenty women and children and destroying dwellings. "This would not be reckoned a very generous manly way of annoying the Enemy after a Declaration of War: how much to be condemned then in a time of Peace If you have no authority over these Indians, but look upon them as an Independent People I shall be glad to be informed of it & must go into some other method of obtaining satisfaction."

LaJonquière replied that Governor Phips was "very fortunate in being able to control" his Indians. Those living in Canada were "free to act as they choose," but he will direct the French who have bought any captives to return them after the purchase price has been repaid. In other words, if you ransom our captives you can have them.

Henry Thayer's 1898 paper before the Maine Historical Society provides illuminating details on the fates of the captives, but also sheds light on the financial transactions made by the Indigenous People with their English captives. It was nearly the end of this profitable business for the Kennebecs and other Wabanaki (Buduswagan) tribes in the Dawnland.

Over the next year the captives were sold in Canada or escaped. Timothy Whidden and Hannah Holmes were redeemed and later married. Solomon Whidden escaped to Quebec, where he died of an illness. Philip Jenkins also died of an illness.

Captain Phineas Stevens, agent for the recovery of captives received a formal accounting of the Swan Island captives from officials in Quebec. "A List of the English Prisoners which the Abenakis Indians have brought to Quebec. The St. Francois Indians to the number of forty have struck near Richmond Fort to Revenge the death of an Abenakis chief which the English have killed near Boston & have brought to this City the Prisoners which they have sold to the French who was willing to buy them."

Stevens reported he was told "Some of the People who had bought them were poor & would Expect there money as Soon as the prisoners were taken from them."

One of the first to be ransomed was Timothy Whitten [Wheaton]. Stevens had not brought cash with him so he "Borrowed of Colo. Lydius" 315 livres to pay for him and gave his note to Lydius for that sum. Whitten reached Boston in April 1751 without "one Penny of Money to pay his charges" and asked and received three pounds from the government.

Stevens received £18.7.6 to reimburse him for his note to Lydius.

The Boston *News-Letter* of April 4 carried this story: "Yesterday came from Quebeck Capt. Phineas Stevens, which place he left 25 February last. He brought with him Timothy Wheaten, whose brother Solomon died in Canada as did Philip Jenkins. As to the rest (being 18 in number) he informs that the French Governor has promised to send to Crown Point this Spring, to tarry till their ransoms are paid."

Timothy married Hannah Holmes, another former captive in September, after she was ransomed for 250 livres.

The Massachusetts government told the relatives of the captives that they should raise the money for their loved ones' ransoms.

Lazarus Noble, Jabez Chubb, John Ross, Abigail Noble, Hanna Holmes, William Ross, John Noble, Maria Noble and Benjamin Noble were all bought by Frenchmen and women and returned to Massachusetts. Philip Jenkins was bought but died at the hospital on October 28, 1750. The amounts paid ranged from 124 livres for William Ross to 382.15 livres for Mrs. Abigail Noble.

The French livre was worth about 10 ½ pence sterling. If the average price for an adult was 200 livres, the average cost in English money was £8. 15 shillings. In 1723 Massachusetts offered to pay £100 for an adult male over twelve and £50 for women and children. Governor Shirley in 1755 reduced this to £40 for men and £20 for women and children. Still this was the equivalent of nearly two years wages for a working man.

John Martin gave his promissory note for 260 livres to the French Governor General and was allowed to return. Solomon Whidden (Whitney, Wheaton) escaped from the Indians but died in a hospital on November 18, 1750. As of February 1, 1752, according to Nathaniel Wheelwright, Seth Webb, Joseph Chandler and Joseph Noble were still at St. François; Mathew Noble had been purchased by S. Amiol and not returned; Frances Noble had been bought by Mr. St. Ange and was still in Montreal.

According to this report, the Kennebecs had been joined in the raids by warriors from the St. François, Algonquins and Becancour tribes. All had sold their captives in Canada for money and equivalents in clothes.

Ten captives from Swan's Island were returned in May 1751 via Crown Point: Lazarus and Abigail Noble and four of their children, John , Mary, Matthew, Benjamin; the Noble's servants, Jabez Chubb and Hannah Holmes; William Ross and his son John. The Nobles' children, Joseph, Frances and Abigail were left behind.

The Nobles returned to Swan island with their four children.

Stevens and Wheelwright returned to Canada in 1752 seeking to redeem more captives and successfully retrieved eight including Lambert and Whitney from New Meadows and Samuel Webb of Windham.

They could find information on thirteen remaining in Canada. Six chose to stay or the Abenakis refused to give them up. These included youngsters "Joseph Noble, Daniel Mitchell, John Forster taken by the Abenakis of St. François, who are obstinately set on keeping them, whatever solicitation Mons Rigaud de Vaudreuill could use, they having adopted them."

Solomon Mitchell, the eldest son of Mitchell of North Yarmouth "about twelve years old, absolutely resolved to stay at Mountryal Sieur Des Pins and Mons Longueuil did not think he ought to force him away against his will."

Mitchell and Noble later went to Canada to try and retrieve their children, but they were forced to return home without their children. Attempts by Governor Phips also failed to bring back the children. The French Commander DuQuesne told Phips he had no control over Indians because they were not "prisoners of war" but "slaves fairly sold." DuQuesne added:"Nothing so difficult as to get slaves from them, especially when they have distributed them among their wigwams to make up for their dead."

According to Henry Thayer writing in 1898, Joseph (eight when captured) and Abigail (a baby when captured) remained in Canada with their Native families. Frances Noble was baptized in 1753 and remained for eleven years with the St. Ange Chaily family in Montreal who had paid 300 livres for her. In 1761 after the fall of Quebec to the English, Captain Samuel Harden found Frances (now named Eleanor or Elaine) in the care of Mon. St. Toise in "a nunnery" on August 24 and brought her back to Boston on October 4. She lived in Boston with a Capt. Wilson until she learned English and then moved to Newbury. In 1776 she married Jonathan Tilton in Hampton and in 1801 John Shute of Newmarket, New Hampshire.

Harden petitioned the Massachusetts General Court for recompense of his expenses, because Noble was "greatly impoverished both as to his Estate and bodily health" and could not contribute to the ransom of his daughter.

Joseph refused to return, and according to Frances, he asked her "not to let it be known where he was, lest he, too, should be obliged to leave his friends and return."

Some of the Whiddens and Nobles returned to Indian Point on the southern end of Swan Island in the Kennebec River. Benjamin and John Whidden sold their land on Swan island in 1770 and moved to Pittston and Fairfield.

The Abenakis' hunt continued the next year with attacks at Fort Richmond, Yarmouth and Falmouth. Six men were captured and one killed in July at New Meadows, while the Kennebecs rampaged through the neighborhood killing cattle and burning dwellings.

Even in the aftermath of these raids in 1750, English settlers began to move north of Fort Richmond in 1751.

Massachusetts formally claimed all land fifty-five miles north of Fort Richmond and within six miles of the repopulated village at Norridgewock. More of the Norridgewock tribe moved up the Kennebec to Canada. And the French Governor DuQuesne voiced the fear that the English would attack Quebec by way of the Kennebec. He urged the Norridgewock to resist the English expansion and sent two priests, Audran and Gaunon, to reinforce the French connection.

And they did.

On July 23, 1751 Phips warned Jabez Bradbury that Lithgow had sent an "account of mischiefs done by a great Number of Indians, & probably divers of the Norridgewocks." The same day Phips told Lithgow "we have so much reason to fear that the Norridgewock are in Confederacy with those of St. Francois."

Two days later Capt. John Gatchel of Brunswick told Colonel Ezekiel Cushing that "yesterday a number of Indians attacked some of our people" at New Meadows near the Kennebec "as they were mowing: & carried Seven Into Captivity viz: Edmund Hinkley, Isaac Hinkley, Gideon Hinkley, Samuel Lumber (Lombard), Samuel Whitney & his son Samuel, Hezekiah Purrenton (Purinton)."

Issac Hinkley's body was later found nearby.

According to Gatchel there were between twenty and thirty Indians. "We are In a Distress Condition & without we are Speedily helped are Afraid must abandon our Settlement."

The Abenaki then moved eastward to Pemaquid and St. Georges rivers, where they were reportedly joined by Penobscots.

Samuel Hinkley later said they were attacked by nineteen Indians, armed with new guns, and one Frenchman about two in the afternoon. He testified that the nine Norridgewock Indians "were more forward for killing all the Captives but were prevented by the other Indians." Hinkley said the Norridgewock Indians "were sett down on Canada River, Supposed to have been drawn there by the Influence of the French."

The men were eventually redeemed from Canada

In 1752 Massachusetts Governor William Shirley warned Secretary Newcastle that the French were occupying the upper reaches of the Kennebec River with plans to build forts there as part of the French plan "to make themselves Masters of the Continent within these last 5 or 6 years." A report that proved to be false.

As part of his defense against the French and their Native allies on the Kennebec, Governor Shirley authorized the building of a string of forts on the Kennebec. Frankfort (then Pownalborough, Dresden) was the site of the stocktake built in 1752 on the lower Kennebec. Called Fort Frankfort and alternately Fort Shirley, it served as a forward supply post and defensive fort on the way to Fort Halifax (now Winslow). Fort Shirley was never attacked, and was garrisoned by the local militia. In 1760-61 the Pownalborough Courthouse was erected on the site of Fort Shirley using most of its timbers. The block house lasted until June 12, 1817, when it was dismantled and Edward Austin built a stonewall "through the middle of the spot on which the blockhouse stood." With the support of Hancock and other Kennebeck Proprietors, Pownalborough became the Shiretown for the new county of Lincoln.

The Pownalborough Courthouse and the home of Thomas and John Hancock's factor, Jonathan Bowman, still stand and are open to the public.

The owners of the Kennebeck Patent were incorporated by the Massachusetts General Court as The Proprietors of the Kennebeck Purchase from the Late Colony of New Plymouth. James and William Bowdoin, Silvester Gardiner, Benjamin Hallowell, Thomas Hancock, John Temple, Charles Apthorp, James Pitts and other investors became the owners of a huge tract along the Kennebec River. The General Court decided that the Kennebeck Proprietors had a legal claim to their land through deeds from the Kennebec tribe. The fort commanders were directed to "keep the Indians quiet." A legislative committee urged the proprietors to give "satisfaction" to the

Natives that would avoid trouble. Out with the Norridgewock tribe, in with the English tribe.

After some delay caused by smallpox and the need to "bring in the Norridgewocks to the treaty, without which there can be no Safety in a treaty with the other Tribes," the English and the Eastern Abenaki renewed the treaty of 1749 in 1753. The outbreak of the French and Indian war the next year shattered that dream.

William Pepperrell led the Massachusetts delegation to Fort Richmond, accompanied by James Bowdoin, Jacob Wendell and William Hubbard. The Kennebeck Proprietors–Bowdoin and Wendell– hoped to convince the Norridgewock to tolerate the increase in settlers brought to the Kennebec by the company.

Quenois led the Kennebec delegation. He wanted Dummer's Treaty enforced, which he asserted that "no settlement should be made above Richmond Fort." Interpreter Walter McFarland then told the Abenaki that they had already sold their land along the Kennebec in the 1640's and 1650's. Moreover, the British claimed the land based on the building of "ancient trading Houses up this River, by ancient Settlements and by ancient Deeds now produced" to the Kennebecs.

The next day Quenois gave the Wabanaki version of "ancient" treaties. In 1713 at Portsmouth "the Indians desired the English might not settle further eastward than Brunswick, which was then settled. We were then bid that if any Englishmen should settle further Eastward," we should "inform the Governor of it, and they should pay dear for it."

The Natives agreed to the settlements at Brunswick, North Yarmouth, Casco-Bay and Saco. Then according to Quenois at the Treaty of Arrowsic in 1717, the Kennebecs had agreed to allow the British to "go as far up the river as Richmond."

Quenois and other Kennebec spokesmen insisted "We have never heard that any of the Governors desired the English might settle higher up than Richmond; although we have heard it from other people."

The Natives stressed the importance of this, but then agreed to accept settlements up to Frankfort. The Kennebecs argued that "You have Land enough below" Frankfurt and we "have but little Space; we desire to live as Brothers."

To the commissioner's assertion that the Indians would keep hunting and fishing rights, the Kennebecs responded that "If the English should settle.. It would drive away our Game, which has been the Case with Respect to the Lands between Richmond and the Sea."

The commissions insisted that the land had been legally purchased and that the Indians had accepted truck houses, which to the English meant settlements. The Indians differentiated between a trading post and a town.

Ultimately, the Kennebecs ratified the 1749 and 1752 treaties and promised to "enquire of our old Men" respecting the sale of the lands.

The peace lasted less than a year.

The Kennebec leaders turned to the French, whose governor, Ange DuQuesne de Menneville promised to provide military supplies to the Indians and build French forts on the Kennebec River–a promise never kept.

The truce was broken when two Wabanaki were killed near Fort St. Georges in 1754. Then some Norridgewock people informed William Lithgow, the commander at Fort Richmond, that the French were building a new fort at the head of the Kennebec. The report turned out to be wrong, but not before Governor Shirley decided to establish a new fort at Taconic Falls on the Kennebec–thirty-seven miles above Fort Richmond. The Kennebeck Proprietors took this opportunity to order the construction of a fortified trading post, called Fort Western, at Cushnoc near present day Augusta. Forts Richmond and Halifax were to be connected by a wagon road–something new on the Kennebec.

Governor Shirley, who had secretly been granted a share in the Kennebeck Company and whose daughter, Harriet, had married a son of Robert Temple, a Kennebeck proprietor, then urged the legislature to end the purchase of lands from "a few Indians" and to stop seeking "their Permission to settle Lands within the undoubted Limits of this Province."

Governor Shirley met with twenty-seven Kennebec men and told them that the English victory at Norridgewock legitimized English ownership of all lands south of that village "by right of Conduct in War." Moreover, "it was interely owing to Kindness" that the Kennebecs had been allowed "your present possessions."

When the Kennebecs protested the forts and settlements, Governor Shirley asserted "I did not ask your consent."

In July the governor led 500 militiamen up the Kennebec. Gerhsom Flagg, a member of the Plymouth Company, led a work party of 12 carpenters, one teamster, one cook and 3 masons to build Fort Western at Cushnoc, based on the Plymouth Company directions. "A house of hewn timber not less than ten inches thick, one hundred feet long, thirty two feet wide, and sixteen high for the reception of the said Province stores, with conveniences for lodging the soldiers placed there by the government; and will picquet in the same at thirty feet distance from every part of said house, and build a blockhouse of twenty-four feet square at the two opposite angles."

They then moved further up the river, but found no French fort. Then they built Fort Halifax at the Taconic Falls, where the Sebasticook River enters the Kennebec. The fort was 100 feet long and forty feet wide with room for 400 troops. It had flankers and blockhouses and cannon redoubts on a small hill. This fort was only a few miles from the reestablished Norridgewock village, causing many of the Abenakis to move to Canada.

In the fall of 1754, William Lithgow was left with 120 men to garrison the new fort.

Both forts Violated the treaties between the Abenaki and English.

The remaining conciliatory Indians remained and told Colonel Winslow, the commander at Fort Halifax (now the town of Winslow), that they desired to live in peace.

The French Governor DuQuesne recalled the two priests, Audran and Gaunon, and urged the Norridgewock people to move to Canada. At the same time he promised guns and supplies to the Abenaki, Maliseet and Mi'kmaq warriors if they would attack Fort Halifax.

On a macro scale, Governor Shirley pushed for a British intercolonial conference to better organize the colonies to confront the French. Bowdoin was a representative from Massachusetts. The Albany Conference of 1754 adopted a plan proposed by Benjamin Franklin to form the colonies into a formal union with military and civil powers. The so-called Albany Plan is considered the first proposed independent union of the American colonies. Neither the English Crown nor Parliament approved. But war had already begun in western Pennsylvania, thanks to George Washington and his band of Virginia militia.

CHAPTER FOUR
THE FINAL ABENAKI AND ENGLISH WAR ALONG THE KENNEBEC

Back on the Kennebec. In October 1754 more than 100 Abenaki and former Norridgewock warriors from the Canadian villages came down the Kennebec to attack Fort Halifax.

On October 30 they surprised six soldiers cutting lumber outside Fort Halifax killing and scalping one and capturing four.

One of the captives was Silas Whitemarsh, who was taken to Canada, where he remained.

The subsequent attack on the fort failed and they returned to Canada.

As a result, an angry Governor Shirley withheld the presents of supplies promised to the Norridgewock and Penobscot tribes in the Eastern District and reinforced the garrisons at the forts.

The General Court raised more troops; offered £100 for the scalp of a St. François Indian and £10 for a captive. Fort Halifax was to be strengthened and supplied with mortars and men. Jedediah Preble was appointed the commander of Fort Halifax.

Before Preble and the forty recruits could arrive, William Lithgow reported on January 9, 1755, that "the soldiers of Fort Halifax are in a most deplorable condition for want of shoes, bedding and bodily clothing." The men lacked snowshoes and supplies were down to one month. They must provide oxen and sleds to move supplies from Fort Richmond and Fort Western to Halifax, wrote Lithgow. A great many of the men were sick, according to Lithgow and "our Doctor has left us." In the spring, flat bottom boats will be needed to move supplies up the river, wrote Lithgow. Governor Shirley, then, ordered a supply boat to the Kennebec and directed that Major Samuel Denny and General John Watts send supplies from Arrowsic.

Lithgow told Shirley in a February 21, 1755, letter "that a party of French and Indians will attack this fort in the spring." Later in 1755 Lithgow erected three redoubts on hills around the fort which was a 117 foot square.

Both sides prepared for a renewal of war in the spring.

Fearing war, the Penobscots remaining in the Dawnland moved even further up their river.

New raids along the Kennebec in the spring of 1755, brought a full declaration of war from Massachusetts on all Abenakis except the remaining Penobscots on the river.

Massachusetts Lieutenant Governor Spencer Phips in 1755 authorized all of "His Majesty's subjects of this Province to Embrace all opportunities of pursuing, captivating, killing and Destroying all and every" Wabanaki Indian. Most settlers interpreted this as reinforcing their approach that did not discriminate between peaceful and hostile Indians. Genocide was on the table.

Along the Kennebec the Natives burned dwellings in New Boston (now Gray). Then on May 13, they killed two men at Frankfort (now Dresden). The Indians moved on to the Sheepscot where they captured five men out plowing. Mr. Barrett was shot at Taconic Falls. Mr. Wheeler was captured near Fort Halifax. John Tufts and Abner Marston were captured near Fort Shirley in Dresden. And two men, Jonathan Farwell and Joseph Tailor (Taylor), were captured near New Gloucester. Both men were brought to Canada and sold to Frenchmen, but were later ransomed.

A Mr. Wheeler was captured while traveling between forts Western and Halifax.

A Mr. Snow was killed after killing an Indian near present day Paris. His companion Samuel Butterfield was captured and later ransomed. The Reverend Smith reported on June 20: "We have news that one Snow was found killed on the back of North Yarmouth and another man with him was taken."

With war all but declared, the Massachusetts government finally declared war on all of the Eastern Indians except the Penobscots on June 11. The bounties were raised from £100 to 250 for a scalp and from £110 to 250 for a captive. In other words, death was as good as alive.

In June 1755 the Abenaki attacked Fort St. Georges and killed two sons of John Brown in a marsh that is now part of Warren, leading Massachusetts authorities to demand that the conciliatory Penobscots at Fort St. Georges leave hostages before returning to Penobscot.

But before the Natives could leave, militia men and scalp hunters ambushed the Penobscots encamped at Owls Head killing twelve or fourteen, and scalping nine for the £250 bounty.

On July 1 as part of the attack at Owls Head, "rangers" from Newcastle killed the friendly Margaret Moxa, her infant child, and her husband.

Capt. James Cargil, commander of the Rangers, was later tried for the murder of Margaret and acquitted. Presents and a letter of apology were sent to Margaret's family. Not surprisingly, the peaceful Penobscots around Fort St. Georges were angry and frustrated. They complained to acting governor, Spencer Phips, who replied on August 18, 1755: "Our People cannot distinguish between your tribe" and the hostile Indians so they should move close to Fort St. Georges. If they did not, Phips said they would "be destroyed" and "the blame will be upon you."

In the big picture, General Edward Braddock with thousands of regular British troops was being soundly defeated by the French and Indians near Fort Duquesne near what is now Pittsburg, Pennsylvania.

At the same time a British force was defeating the French in Acadia/ Nova Scotia, driving the French forces back to Fort Louisbourg.

In September the Abenaki in Canada came down the Kennebec bypassed Fort Halifax and attacked settlers along the St. Georges River on September 24. One was killed and many cattle killed.

The Massachusetts government then offered to pay the Penobscots to fight against the French and the Canadian Natives and promised to protect them if they surrendered. The conciliatory Penobscots refused.

On November 5 convinced that the Penobscots were responsible, the Massachusetts government declared war on the Penobscots forcing more Penobscot and Kennebec people to flee to Maliseet villages along the St. John River in far eastern Dawnland.

Those members of the Kennebec and Penobscot tribes remaining in the Eastern District refused to ally with either the French or the English. But English hostilities and the lack of supplies from the English, forced many of the Kennebec people to move to Canada or sympathize/support their fellow tribal people in that country.

Meanwhile raids continued along the Maine frontier in 1756 and 1757.

In the winter of 1756 the colonial governors and military leaders meeting in New York decided on an ambitious plan for that year's campaigns. Two thousand men would travel up the Kennebec and Chaudiere rivers to attack the French and Indian settlements; ten thousand men would attack Crown Point; six thousand troops would march to Niagara; and two thousand men would have another try on Fort Duquesne.

The Massachusetts General Court balked at raising the necessary taxes. The expedition up the Kennebec River was the first to go. The Massachusetts government raised 300 men as rangers in the Eastern District and Commissary General John Wheelwright at Wells was ordered to accumulate supplies for the Kennebec expedition.

Before anything could be done, the Abenaki warriors attacked Fort St. Georges. The fort was strong, but on March 24 two men were killed and a third scalped but lived. A man was captured but escaped to warn the settlements westward to the Kennebec and beyond.

On May 9 warriors attacked the fortified house of Thomas Means (Meaks) at Flying Point (now Freeport). Means was killed as was one of his children. Mrs. Means' sister, Molly Finney, was carried off by the natives. In Canada she was sold as a servant/slave to a farmer, until she was rescued by Captain McClellan of Falmouth. They were later married. One warrior was killed by Means' boarder.

This attack was vividly described in the *Boston Gazette* of May 24, 1756. "A vessel arrived last Thursday from Merecocheague Neck the master informed That on the 9th Inst just at the Break of Day 5 Indians beset the House of one Meaks went up Chamber and haul'd him, his wife and Child out of Bed; after which (while the Woman was suckling her Child) the inhuman Blood-thirsty Wretches fired and kill'd the child which cut part of the Woman's Breast off. They fired then and kill'd the Man, and as they shot his wife and took her Sister Prisoner; a Young Man being in the upper Chamber and hearing the Noise loaded his Gun, fir'd and kill'd one Indian when the other 4 run off and left the Woman and the dead without Scalping them."

The Abenaki raiders then broke into small parties, attacking isolated settlements and settlers from Harpswell to the Kennebec to North Yarmouth.

Nearby, Abijah Young was also wounded and captured on May 9. He was rescued about a year later but died of smallpox.

On Arrowsic Island Natives killed a Mr. Preble and captured his three young children, who were later ransomed by Captain Harnden of Woolwich.

The scouting parties sent out by the province of Massachusetts had little apparent effect. Two soldiers from Fort Halifax were killed by Kennebec Indians while fishing near the fort.

Scouting parties sent up the Kennebec and Androscoggin rivers returned empty handed.

When Great Britain declared war on France in June, the ministry in London took over the management of the war. Governor Shirley, who had held his post since 1740 was recalled and later dispatched to Bermuda.

General Montcalm captured several British forts along the line of New York and the Great Lakes.

The English began to further restrict supplies to the Eastern Natives, further forcing them to ally with the French even though many wanted to remain neutral and peaceful.

As 1757 opened, both the English settlers and the Indigenous tribes in the Dawnland were "gloomy" about the future, according to the historian, William Williamson.

In Boston in January the English, led by Lord Loudoun, decided that this year they would concentrate on capturing Louisbourg. A concept that failed when the British found out they were outmanned and outgunned on land and in the ocean. The French General Montcalm captured Fort William Henry and 3000 English soldiers.

Again, the Massachusetts General Court settled on 250 rangers (Indian hunters) who would patrol from Salmon Falls eastward through the Kennebec to St. Georges River. Two provincial warships would patrol the coast.

The Native tribesmen having returned from their winter hunting grounds in the interior or their villages in Canada renewed their scattered attacks on the English settlements and forts.

In early April Captain Joshua Freeman arrived at Fort St. Georges with a small party of rangers.

When several Penobscots led by Neptune arrived at the fort under a flag of truce to trade, Freeman's men grabbed one Indian and brought him into the fort. The Natives returned under a flag of truce and Captain Jabez Bradbury released the captive. That night Freeman's men went out to find the Indians and managed to kill one before retreating to the fort. Although there was no major fight, the Penobscots remained in the neighborhood ambushing men who went out to fish or hunt. Three men were killed and scalped–Robert Kye, Joseph and Henry Handley. And Mrs. Thompson was captured while milking her cows. Her husband later ransomed her for $40.

Near Pleasant Point a party of Frenchmen and Natives killed John Watson and captured William Watson and a Mr. Larrabee.

The English were not without their own raids. Captain Remily of the Broad Bay scouts, reported in June that Captain Joseph Cox of the St. Georges Company brought in two scalps from a raid on Owls Head. The Reverend Thomas Smith noted in his diary on June 18: "I received £165 and £33 of Cox, my part of scalp money." Praise the Lord, and collect the scalp money.

As usual the Natives found their way around the patrols. On May 18 Kennebec and Androscoggin (Anasagunticooks) ambushed Captain Lithgow near Fort George. In the skirmish two English soldiers were killed, several wounded and at least two Abenaki warriors were killed.

In early June Abenaki warriors overran the house of Ebenezer Hall on Matinicus. The Penobscots had complained for several years that Hall interfered with their hunting seals and waterfowl on the island. Hall had ignored a 1753 order from the General Court to leave the island. Four years later, Hall was killed and scalped and his wife, Marah, and four children, Sarah, Peter, Phebe and Tabitha, were carried into captivity to Penobscot and on to Canada. There Captain Andrew Watkins paid 215 livres for her and sent her to England, from where she ultimately returned to Maine. Her children were never accounted for even by the persistent Emma Coleman.

Close to the Kennebec, a Mr. Hopkins was killed and a Mr. McFarland was captured in Newcastle while threshing wheat on McFarland's barn.

In August 1757, Thomas Pownall, brother of John Pownall, Secretary to the Board of Trade, became governor of Massachusetts.

Captain Bradbury was replaced by John North as commander of Fort St. Georges, and was promptly accused of trading guns and powder to the Indian tribes. Kennebec captains, Lithgow and Howard were called to testify before the legislative committee, but Bradbury was eventually exonerated.

A smallpox epidemic raced through the Eastern District, and was credited by the English as discouraging the Indians from attacking the English settlements. So the summer and fall of 1757 passed rather quietly in the Dawnland.

The Plymouth Company was authorized to settle 100 families around Fort Halifax.

Governor Pownall gave a fiery speech to the General Court in early 1758 calling for a defensive posture and invoking the wrath of God on the French and Eastern tribes. "Let us save the strength, collect the force, and treasure up the funds and means, of the Province until God shall call them out, one and all, to wreak his vengeance upon the savage violators of amity and peace, and the Perfidious French of Canada."

At the same time, Pownall recommended that only Fort Halifax and a fort on the Penobscot be retained and that forts at Pemaquid and St. Georges be dismantled. That would be enough with scouts to cut off communication with Canada to restrain the "Noridgwaegs, Penobscot and St. John's" who are all the Indian tribes "left in the Eastern parts."

William Pitt became prime minister of Great Britain and promptly called for renewed offensive operations in America against Forts Louisbourg, Ticonderoga and Duquesne.

Massachusetts agreed to raise 7,000 men with reinforcements going to the Kennebec River region: Fort Halifax, 50; Cushnoc, 16; Fort George, 5; and additional troops further up the Kennebec and further east at Forts St. Georges, Broad Bay and Pemaquid.

On July 16 the Fortress of Louisbourg surrendered to the English. Fort Duquesne was occupied by the English and renamed Fort Pitt. The expedition against Ticonderoga failed.

The Kennebec region suffered minor Indian attacks in May and June. William Pomeroy was killed and his son, William, captured near the river at Frankfort on May 11, according to the report of Pheby Pomeroy. On the same day one child of Ezra Davis was captured and brought to Canada. According to Coleman, the children were still in Canada in 1761.

Indians captured English settlers at Friendship (Meduncook) and the Sheepscot in late May and early June.

Then on June 8 a couple, Ebenezer and Mary (Harnden) Preble, were killed on Arrowsic Island near Georgetown and their six children, Rebecca, Samuel, Mehetable, Ebenezer, Mary and William, and a servant, Sarah Fling, were captured. The infant William and the servant lad were also killed. Sarah may have died on the march to Canada.

According to a monument in Georgetown marking the burial spot of Ebenezer and Mary, this was "The last Massacre of the Indian Wars on the Kennebec."

The story is told by Sameul Harnden, Mary's father from Woolwich, in a May 27, 1761, petition to the General Court.

"That on June 8th his son-in-law, Ebenezer Preble when he was in his field at George Town, now Woolwich, was shot dead by a party of four Indians, who afterward attacked his house, wherein was his wife, six children, his servant girl and a servant lad. Mary, his wife (and the petitioner's eldest daughter) for sometime defended the house, but at last, she was shot dead through the door or window. The Indians then entered, plundered the house, and carried off the six children, namely: Rebecca, the eldest about eleven years old, Samuel, Mehitabel, Ebenezer, Mary and a sucking infant about three months old named William. Also the servant girl, Sarah Fling, and the servant lad.

"The girl was wounded but survived, the young infant they killed, the lad they wounded mortally and then knocked him in the head so that he dyed. The other five children and the girl they carried to Quebec and sold to the French.

"That in the year 1759, after the reduction of Quebec, Rebecca and Mary were accidentally discovered, known and challenged there in the hands of the remaining French inhabitants, by William Nicholls and Alexander Campbell, who belonged to the eastern parts of this province, and they, borrowing one hundred dollars from Col. Robert Moncton, obtained their release, and accordingly the said two children came home to their paternal grandfather, Jonathan Preble, yeoman, who afterward asked the Court for thirty pounds, two shillings and eleven pence for he is 'not able to bear the charge of such redemption, being old, opprest with the calamities of war, infirm and poor;' he hath advanced to the said Campbell the sum above said but that, he should have thought himself obliged to do, in justice, and gratitude to a man who had restored two of his grandchildren to him even tho he had not left to himself a single penny to support him after.

The child Mehitable was carried to old France to attend to her French mistress and was to return back with her to Quebeck, as he knows off. The servant girl has not been heard off since August."

Harnden went on to fear that the other children were detained in Canada "where without doubt the practice and principals of the Popish religion will be instilled into them in their tender years and propagated during their lives if not recovered."

Harnden was given money by the General Court to go to Canada to rescue his grandchildren, which he did in the summer of 1761. He managed to find Samuel, Frances Noble and Ebenezer, redeemed them and brought them back to Massachusetts.

Mehitable may have remained in France, but the French asserted she was not with M. Mournier at Rochelle and may have remained in Montreal.

Mary died unmarried in Woolwich and Rebecca married Thomas Motherwell.

That summer Nathaniel Winslow and his sons, Nathan, John and Elisha of Damariscotta were captured by Natives while fishing off Matinicus. Two of the crew of eight were killed and the rest brought to St. John River, where Nathaniel escaped. In November 1759 the General Court awarded him seven pounds.

The conciliatory Norridgewock faction on the Kennebec moved to Canada in the summer of 1758.

The French and their Penobscot and Maliseet allies made their last attempt to clear the Eastern District in the late summer of 1758. On August 26, 1758, fifty French soldiers and 250 Maliseet and Penobscot warriors attacked Fort St. Georges. They failed, but roving bands destroyed homes and cattle.

The French complained that the Natives were "unwilling to go fight unless we feed their women and children."

Governor Pownall decided in 1759 to move the most eastern English fort into the heart of the Penobscot tribe. The main British army was to move north through Ticonderoga and Crown Point and meet General Wolfe at Quebec. General Amherst encouraged Pownall to mount an expedition to the Penobscot, because with the Kennebec and St. John rivers firmly closed by the English, the Penobscot was the Abenakis' and the French's only access to the ocean.

Forts Halifax and Western were given extra troops, but Pownall and four hundred men sailed for the Penobscot in early May. They faced no opposition from the Native tribe, and constructed Fort Pownall on the western side of the river, now Prospect.

Pownall then went up the river beyond the tidal point, and sent a message to the Native leaders that any opposition would result in their destruction. But they could peacefully live near the fort and enjoy their hunting, fishing and planting grounds.

However, the seeds of future English settlements were present with Pownall in the person of Samuel Waldo whose claim to the Muscongus and Waldo patents led him to mark a spot near the river (now Bangor) as the eastern end of his proprietorship. Waldo died on the spot after making his assertion, but his family soon would bring settlers to the Penobscot and force the Natives far above the tidal line of the river.

Pownall would soon brag that Fort Pownall was the most defensible in the province, and that he had extended English power over land that had been for "long a den for savages, and a lurking place for renegade Frenchmen."

Before the end of the fighting season the English had captured Niagara, Ticonderoga, Crown Point and Quebec. In October Robert Rogers, who would later command a company of British rangers in the American Revolution, and his rangers assaulted the Eastern Native strongholds of St. François and Becancour. Many of the Natives who had fled north from the Kennebec were killed and wounded. Several English captives were freed. The substantial villages of the Abenaki were ransacked and destroyed.

That section of Arrowsic (Georgetown) that had experienced so many Abenaki attacks, was formally incorporated as the town of Woolwich (Nauseag or Nequasset).

During the winter forts Halifax and Cusnoc were manned on the Kennebec, along with forts St. Georges and Pownall. With French power virtually removed from eastern North America, no real hostilities were expected and none were experienced.

The closure of forts George, Frankfurt (Shirley) and Richmond marked the end of English and French/Native conflict along the Kennebec that had lasted more than a century.

After the fall of Quebec in September 1760, New Englanders believed their frontier nightmare was at last over. The source of strength for the Eastern Natives and the provider of commerce for English captives was done. "Quebec, after repeated struggles and efforts is at length reduced: Quebec I had almost called it that Pandora's box, from whence unnumber'd plagues have issued for more than one hundred years, to distress, to enfeeble, to lay waste, these northern colonies; and which might, perhaps in the end have proved fatal to them!," gloated the Reverend Jonathan Mayhew from his pulpit. No doubt thinking with his congregation "God is great."

Fearing unrest and hoping to rekindle the fur trade on the Kennebec, Massachusetts in 1761 sent a ranger unit under James

Howard of Cushnoc up the Kennebec to the Chaudiere River. No trade or conflicts resulted.

The Wabanaki tribes were destroyed by the war. The British victory deprived the tribes of the Dawnland of their French ally.

The Kennebecs, Pigwackets and Androscoggins never recovered. Virtually all tribal organizations were gone in Maine and Canada. Small family bands of Kennebecs roamed the river valley. Jacob Bailey, minister at Pownalborough, reported in 1766 that "a great number of Indians frequent this neighborhood. They are remnant oif the ancient Tribe and lead a rambling life." He described them as "very savage in their Dress and Manners" and "have a great Aversion to the English Nation."

English settlers flooded the Dawnland. There were now more than 23,000 English settlers in Maine occupying properties in the Dawnland. Many settled without regard to Abenaki land claims or the ownership claims of the great proprietors like the Kennebeck Company. With so many European settlers, the Abenaki could no longer hunt or live their nomadic lives. They could no longer obtain supplies from the French. They could no longer take refuge in Canada. They could no longer sell captives. They could no longer obtain furs to trade. The Eastern tribes could no longer protect their homelands or even support their dwindling population. The military and economic power of the Wabanaki tribes was broken.

The dispossession of the Kennebec Tribe was almost complete, but the life of the Kennebec settlers was still hard. Poverty in the Maine rural areas was widespread. Reverend Jacob Bailey, the local Anglican minister at West Pownalborough (now Dresden), later wrote: "I might here add many affecting instances of their extreme poverty—that multitudes of children are obliged to go barefoot through the whole winter, with hardly clothes to over their nakedness—that half the houses were without any chimneys—that many people had not other beds than a heap of straw—and whole families had scarce anything to subsist upon, for months together except potatoes, roasted in the ashes."

However, the bright light was that the physical, violent conflict between the Abenaki and English had ended.

But it was not an end to conflict along the Kennebec.

CHAPTER FIVE
THE REVOLUTIONARY FINALE

The end of the war in 1763 brought a finish to major conflicts between the Abenaki and the English along the Kennebec River in the Dawnland. The power of the Abenaki tribes was gone. The Indigenous People were scattered. Most had long since moved to Canada, where they had been further dislocated. The remnants could be found here and there in the Eastern District. There were no more Norridgewock strongholds. Only the Penobscots, Passaquoddies, and Maliseets held onto vestiges of their territory along the Penobscot, St. John and St.Croix rivers.

Governor Francis Bernard's survey of the Native population in the Eastern District in 1764 counted "probably more than 30" warriors on the Kennebec. In other parts of the district, the Penobscot Tribe was listed "at least 60" warriors and the Passamaquody "at least 30."

The same census recorded 23,683 White people and 332 Black people in the organized counties of York, Cumberland and Lincoln. However, there were many uncounted residents in the unorganized regions.

In quick order Windham, Buxton, Bowdoinham, Topsham, Gorham, Boothbay, Bristol, Hallowell, Winslow, Winthrop and Vassalborough were incorporated. Shortly thereafter, the Massachusetts General Court ordered the surveying of twelve townships east of the Penobscot River. The European population was exploding and civil governments replaced the unregulated interior territories along the Kennebec River.

Even though the governor said that the Eastern Abenaki were in constant communication with the Abenaki residents in Canada, they hardly posed a threat to the English settlers. More likely the Indians were in more danger from the settlers. Such an incident occurred near Fort Pownall when four English hunters fired on and killed two Native hunters and stole their furs and traps.

The remaining forts, Halifax and Western, were abandoned in 1766 and 1769.

The French had been thoroughly defeated. The English ruled the eastern seaboard from Newfoundland to Florida.

But soon conflict would return to the Kennebec. But this time it would be Anglo-Americans against their British governors. The fears of the French that the Kennebec River would be a direct avenue of attack against Montreal and Quebec would become reality. But it would not be the French and their Indian allies under the guns of the English.

Violence preceded the actual outbreak of war on the Kennebec. After the Boston Tea Party, the British government tried to bully the Massachusetts radicals into submission with four laws known as the Coercive Acts. In retaliation the Committees of Correspondence in June 1774 urged Americans to join a Solemn League and Covenant to voluntarily refuse to join any economic activity with Great Britain. This brought on often violent conflict between Loyalists and Patriots in the Kennebec region as well as the rest of Massachusetts. Patriots demanded an immediate boycott of British goods, while the Loyalists or Tories demanded denunciations of the Solemn League and Covenant.

Violence was inevitable.

Samuel Goodwin described the situation in Pownalborough to Massachusetts Governor Thomas Gage in an August 10, 1774, letter. "A Number who have Signed, Refuse to have any Connection with those that have not, and would Distroy them that have not, both root and Branch, if in their Power."

In Woolwich the opponents burned one paper covenant, the proponents drew up another and forced the opponents to sign. The minister in Georgetown signed the covenant and then burned it. The Reverend Jacob Bailey, who later became a notorious Tory and was forced to flee, urged his parishioners not to sign with the admonition: "Loyalty to our King and Due Obedience to the Laws."

Bailey reported that in September 1774 "A furious mob at Georgetown was running about in search of tea and compelling people by force of arms to sign the solemn leagues." John Jones was thrown into the Kennebec to force him to sign, according to Bailey.

"They seized Captain [John] Carleton of Woolwich and having prepared a coffin commanded him to dig his own grave, but allowed him to escape," stated Bailey. He added that in Topsham "a Mister Wilson was buried to the chin in sand" and left to be found by his friends or relatives.

Early on Bath residents traveled to Wiscasset to tar and feather a leading Tory and ride him around on a rail. As an added benefit they took 700 pounds of lead from his stores.

Some towns hedged their bets. Abraham Preble, speaking for Bowdoinham, told Governor Gage in an August 3, 1774, letter, that the town refused to signed the covenant but: "No Sir we Value them [our liberties] as our Lives, But we would faine have them Continued to us by Some more Reagular Stream than what we think these Covenants or any thing of that Nature is like to do." In other words no outside interference and that also includes you.

More radical action soon followed, led by men like Samuel Thompson of Brunswick. A well-to-do tavern owner, land speculator and town official, Thompson led armed Patriot mobs through Wiscasset, Georgetown and Pownalborough. In Powalborough Reverend Bailey fled, others were treated to old fashioned dunkings (water torture) and others forced to dig their own graves before they were roughed up and cast aside. In the fall of 1774 they forced the magistrates sitting at the Inferior Court to sign the covenant and reject any new commissions from Governor Gage.

Thompson soon became an appointed agent of the new Massachusetts Provincial Congress in enforcing the Association embargo ordered by the Continental Congress. Thompson was sent to Georgetown in early April 1775 to stop the British mast master, Edward Parry, from dispatching a ship loaded with masts for the British Navy from the Kennebec River. The Georgetown officers seized Parry and refused to turn him over to Thompson, who wanted to use him as bait to lure in the British sloop *Canceaux*. Word of the outbreak of fighting at Concord and Lexington reached Georgetown on April 23. Parry was jailed but was allowed to post bond to appear before the Provincial Congress.

Two years later, British Commodore George Collier commanding *HMS Rainbow* arrived in the Kennebec area to retrieve the same masts left by Parry. A French vessel was loading the masts on the Sheepscot when Collier arrived. Collier's men initially seized the sloop but the local militia responded so forcefully that Collier had to sail his frigate into the river to rescue his men.

Some locals wanted to allow Collier to take the schooner and masts in order to avoid more fighting. The Third Regiment of Lincoln County soon lined the shore and small boats forced Collier to flee down river leaving the French schooner and the masts behind.

Back to 1775. Thompson then left the Kennebec moving westward to Falmouth, where the British sloop was anchored. With a contingent of Kennebec militiamen, Thompson seized Henry Mowatt, the commander of the *Canceaux* when he was ashore. "Thompson's War" became a standoff, when a Falmouth official, fearing that the British ship would destroy the town, refused to put Mowatt in jail.

By May 10 Falmouth leader Enoch Freeman was writing to the Provincial Congress asking for help because "We are in confusion" and "nobody seems to be rational." Hundreds of militiamen arrived in Falmouth to support Thompson, but the town fathers agreed to release Mowatt with Freeman and Jedediah Preble standing surety.

Thompson then returned home after the militia harassed the tories, convincing many to flee when Mowatt and his ship left the harbor. Thompson may have received a temporary setback, but within a year the Massachusetts government had appointed him a brigadier general commanding the militia of Lincoln County.

Unfortunately for Falmouth, Mowatt returned on October 18, 1775, bombarded the town and destroyed most of the buildings and the local ships and shipping industry. It would be a long time before Falmouth (Portland) regained its former prosperity and prominence.

When the American Revolutionary War began in 1775, the Americans hoped for some help or neutrality on the part of the various Native tribes. "We think the Indians will not be disposed to engage in this unhappy quarrel unless deceived and deluded by misrepresentations and this, with Vigilence and care on our part can be prevented," echoed the New York Delegates to the Continental Congress on June 10, 1775.

John Adams, representing Massachusetts in the Continental Congress, wrote to James Warren on June 7, 1775, that "The Nations of Indians inhabiting the Frontiers of the Colonies, are numerous and warlike. They seem disposed to Neutrality."

Adams went on to decry how "The French disgraced themselves last War, by employing them. To let loose these Blood Hounds to scalp Men, and to butcher Women & Children is horrid." Yet it would not be long before the Massachusetts General Court and the Continental Army sought to recruit hundreds of Indians from the tribes in the Eastern District of Maine and Nova Scotia.

The Massachusetts Provincial legislature wasted little time in trying to gain support from the Eastern Indians sending them a long letter of May 10, 1775, promising support with supplies, guns and powder and seeking to enlist warriors in the American cause.

The Anglo-Americans continued to overestimate the power of the Abenaki tribes.

"Brothers, the great wickedness of such as should be our friends but are now our enemies, we mean the ministry of great Britain, have laid deep plots to take away our liberty, and your liberty, they want to get all our money, make us pay it to them when they never earnt it, to make you & us their servants & let us have nothing to eat, drink or ware but what they say we shall, and prevent us from having guns & powder to use to kill our Dear and Wolves & other game, or to send to you to kill your game with and to get skins & fur to trade with us for what you want. But we hope soon to be able to supply you with both guns and Powder of our own making."

The letter continues with the information that Colonel Thomas Goldthwait, commander at Fort Pownall since 1763 "has given up Fort Pownall into the hands of our enemies. We are angry at it & we hear you are angry with him & we dont wonder at it. We want to know what you our good Brothers want from us of Cloathing or warlike stores & we will Supply you as fast as we can."

The British took the cannons from Fort Pownall and then American troops burned the buildings and filled in the ditches in 1775.

The Massachusetts government "hope none of your men or the Indians in Canada will join with our enemies."

The government had enlisted Stockbridge Indians "for one blanket & a Ribband & they will be paid when they are home in the Service and if any of you are willing to list we will do the same for you."

"We have sent Captain John Lane to you for that purpose and he will show you his orders for raising one Company of your men to join us in the war with your & our Enemies."

The Indigenous People still residing in the Eastern District had no intentions of fighting on either side.

Even those in Canada were reluctant to join the British. On August 14, 1775, several St. François warriors arrived at Washington s

Cambridge Headquarters and according to Washington"s August 15 letter to Philip Schuyler: "Several Indians of the tribe of St. Francis came in here yesterday, and confirm the former (Benedict Arnold) accounts of the good Dispositions of the Indian Nations and Canadians to the Interests of America."

Joseph Reed reported in an August 14, 1775, letter that the conference of officers suggested to Swashan, a chief of the St. François tribe that he volunteer with General Schuyler because they had "no occasion" for his services.

Swashan declared to a committee of the Provincial Congress: "As our ancestors gave this Country to you we would not have you destroyed by England; but are ready to afford you assistance."

Stephen Jones, a trader in Machias, summed up the divisions among the Natives. "The Whig and Tory principles run high among the tribes, but the Whig Indians being much the most numerous, the Tories remained at home as neutrals."

During the war the Massachusetts government would spend considerable time and money trying to keep the Natives along the Penobscot and St. John rivers neutral, if not allied with the Americans.

During the war British naval vessels would often sail into the Kennebec for fresh water, wood, cattle, hogs and other foodstuffs. Sometimes they paid and sometimes they did not. Parker Reed recounts a humorous story of an unnamed "old man" who "sold" goods to a warship with the promise of pay the next morning. "But the next morning the old gentleman discovered the ship getting under weigh to go to sea. He immediately proceeded to the shore, mounted a high ledge, and angrily calling out. 'You Englishmen. You! You Englishmen you! Come ashore and pay what you owe me.' The man of war replied by sending a cannon ball at the enraged man. It struck a smooth, perpendicular ledge immediately below where he was standing and the round print of the ball remains in the rock to this day (1894). The ball was afterwards picked up on the flats at low tide, and was kept in the old timber house of John Parker until it was taken down and lost. In his youthful days this author often saw this ball in this house and the indenture in the ledge."

In August 1775 two "British" privateer ships sailed up the Kennebec and anchored at the Eddy in Bath. The local militia under the command of Captain Nathaniel Springer fired on them with cannon and muskets until they slipped their cables and went out with the tide. Reportedly several privateers were killed and wounded. As the Americans chased the ships down river, they were caught in a crossfire and Captain Springer was killed by friendly fire.

Some of the Patriot activity involved the destruction of old fortifications before they could fall into British hands. Fort Frederick at Pemaquid and Fort Pownall on the Penobscot were dismantled. The old fortifications on the Kennebec simply fell into disuse before and during the war.

With two exceptions-the Benedict Arnold Expedition and the Battle of Penobscot Bay–major military activities did not occur in the Eastern District.

The idea of attacking Quebec through the Kennebec river route was hardly new. Indigenous people had used the Kennebec/Dead River route to and from Canada for centuries. In the last war the French had feared that the English would use that route to attack Quebec.

In 1760-1761 British army lieutenant John Montressor even drew a detailed map of the route up the Kennebec to Quebec. A map subsequently used by Arnold.

So when Jonathan Brewer of Waltham first suggested the plan to the Massachusetts Provincial Congress in May 1775, it was not a new plan. But it was rejected. Even Arnold's first proposal on June 15 to the Continental Congress gained little support. Then Arnold traveled to Cambridge to put the concept straight to General George Washington.

He was more receptive, writing on August 20 to General Philip Schuyler about an idea he was mulling. "A Plan of an Expedition, which has engaged my Thoughts for Several Days. It is to penetrate into Canada by Way of Kennebeck River, and so to Quebeck by a Rout ninety miles below Montreal."

Schuyler should attack up the lake chain, and Governor Guy Carleton "must either break up and follow this Party to Quebeck, by which he will leave you a free passage, or he must suffer that important Place to fall into our hands, an Event which would have a decisive effect."

In return Schulyer "wished that the thought had struck you sooner."

And so the Kennebec Expedition was on.

In August Arnold asked Reuben Colburn, who lived on the Kennebec, was a Maine Committee of Safety member and was in Cambridge, to make preparations for the invasion. He was promptly hired to do some preliminary preparation work and provide basic information about the Kennebec--Was there enough material to make boats to travel up the Kennebec? How deep was the water? How long were the portages, and how long was the trip to Quebec?

Colburn lived on the Kennebec in Gardinerston (now Pittsfield) ten miles south of Fort Western.

After his 1761 arrival Colburn was granted 250 acres and operated a sawmill, brick yard and boat yard. His house built in 1765 still stands on Arnold Road just off Route 27 and is a state historical park.

Before he left, Washington gave Colburn money to saw the planks "for the purposes of building batteaux for the use of the Continental Army."

Washington was convinced by the visiting St. François Sachem, Swashan, that "the Indians in Canada in general, and also the French, are greatly in our favor and determined not to act against us. The St. François tribe was an amalgam of Canadian Indians and Kennebec/Norridgewock and Penobscot Natives who had been pushed from the Kennebec River by the English colonists. As an added bonus, Swashan promised "to bring one half of his tribe and had engaged 4 or 5 other tribes if they would be wanted." according to Washington's August 30 letter to Schuyler.

Washington recruited four of Swashan's warriors to act as guides for Arnold. When Arnold reached Swashan's home village, Sartigan on the Chaudiere, he was able to enlist forty warriors from the local tribe. Some may even have been Norridgewock. It is hard to discern what was the motive of Swashan and his tribe in supporting the Americans against the British.

Colburn returned to the Kennebec and enlisted Samuel Goodwin's advice. Goodwin provided a detailed map of the Kennebec and Dead rivers. Major Goodwin was a Kennebeck Proprietor and commander of Fort Shirley and an agent/attorney for the Plymouth Company (aka Kennebeck Proprietors). He and his family moved to the Kennebec in 1756 from Charlestown, and they were first living in Fort Shirley, but when the Pownalborough Courthouse was completed they were the first occupants.

Colburn sent a small scouting party of local residents and a native guide up the river.

Colburn's report to Arnold was very optimistic. The scouts had encountered a Norridgewock, Natanis, who lived on the Dead River. According to the report, Natanis was being paid by General Guy Carleton to spy on the Americans and send him word if the Americans moved up the Kennebec. "We got intelligence of an Indian that he was stationed there by Govr. Charlton as a Spy to watch the motions of an Army, or Spies, that was daily expected from New England; that there was spies on the Head of the Chaudiere River, & down the River some distance there was Stationed a Regular Officer and six Privates," wrote Dennis Getchell and Samuel Barry to Colburn, September 13, 1775.

Arnold later ordered the advance party to kill Natanis on sight. An interesting order, because Washington had given orders not to injure any Cnadians or Indians and not to plunder or insult the inhabitants of Canada. Arnold should punish "all attempts to plunder or insult the inhabitants of Canada'."

Furthermore, "Should any American soldier be so base and infamous, as to injure any Canadian or Indian in his person or property, I do most earnestly enjoin you to bring him to such severe and exemplary punishment, as the enormity of the crime may require—should it extend to death itself, it will not be disproportionate to its guilt at such a time and in such a cause."

Colburn also reported that one "native guide" had learned that the young men of the tribe had gone west into Canada while they were expecting Mohawk warriors to come down the Kennebec to attack the Americans.

As an aside, Colburn was never fully paid for his preparation work and his batteaux, for which his family was still petitioning the federal government in 1824.

When Arnold's little army sailed from Newburyport on September 19, most of Captain Samuel McCobb's Company from the Kennebec area sailed with it. McCobb and his first Lieutenant, Benjamin Patten, were from Georgetown. McCobb had preceded the small fleet to Georgetown to recruit more men. When they arrived at Arrowsic Island, he was there. Most of the sixty-four man company were from the towns of Wiscasset, Woolwich, Pownalborough, Winthrop, and Georgetown.

When Arnold arrived he received Colburn's report and found the batteaux were ready on the Kennebec at Colburn's boatyard at Gardinerston. Colburn had been assisted in building the boats by local men, such as James Winslow, and his son Joanthan.

Meanwhile, Washington had finally notified Congress on September 21 that "I have detached Colonel Arnold with 1000 men to penetrate into Canada by way of Kennebec River and if possible to make himself master of Quebec."

Arnold was unfazed by the report of some hostile Indians and quickly moved his men and supplies in Colburn's batteaux up the river to Fort Western.

Despite the decision of the Continental Congress not to recruit Indians, Arnold offered nine dollars a month (one Portuguese silver dollar and a two dollar bounty), a food allowance and their own officers to any Indians who would join his army. According to Isaac

Senter, the Abenaki promised fifty men and canoes to travel up the Kennebec to Quebec. Arnold would later recruit forty Natives, some of whom were former residents of Norridgewock, when he reached their villages on the Chaudiere.

In late October, the Committee of Congress meeting with Washington, met with "Several Indian Chiefs of the St. Francis, Penobscot, Stockbridge and St. John's Tribes." The delegates noted that they "have been to offer their Services" but were told they would be called if needed, and even wondered if it were "proper" to give them presents.

Arnold's advance party of scouts, including two men from the Merrymeeting Bay, John Getchell, son of Samuel and Sarah (Mariner), and Jeremiah Horne, with knowledge of the river, set off from Fort Western on September 24. According to Arnold's journal, Archibald Steele's men were "to reconnoiter, get all the intelligence he possibly can from the Indians, who, I am informed, are hunting there."

The Americans feared that the Natives would inform the British of their approach, and according to John Henry, "we had been made to believe that this country had numerous Indians in it."

None were encountered, and the advance party reached the Dead River or the western branch of the Kennebec. Several days into the journey they came to the cabin of Natanis on the Dead River. He was not home.

When they came to a fork in the Dead River they found a map in a forked stick, that indicated that people used the eastern fork and marked some Indian encampments. Turned out Natanis was secretly a supporter of the Americans and had left the map for them.

When Arnold reached a French and Indian village of Sartigan where the Famine River enters the Chaudiere, Natanis would be there to greet them. John Henry noted in his journal that Natanis greeted them warmly, and explained that they did wait to meet them on the Dead River because "You would have killed me."

At the headwaters of the Dead River the advance party found an Indian trail that led them over the mountains and down to the Chaudiere River. There they turned back to meet the main body of Arnold's little army.

Meanwhile General Schuyler's force was attacking Montreal. Arnold was far behind in his schedule.

Arnold sent his army out of Fort Western in four sections leaving one day apart. They were led by the men from the scouting party.

Arnold's men made their way without opposition and without seeing any Indians or English soldiers throughout their slow passage up the Kennebec and Dead rivers and over the many carrying spots. It was late in the season. The weather was uncomfortable. Food and supplies ran short. The batteaux made of green wood proved bulky and difficult to carry. A severe Northeaster flooded the rivers and destroyed much of their food and caused the loss of most of the £1,000 in coins that Washington had given Arnold for the expedition's pay and expenses.

Two local Kennebec men, John and Nehemiah Getchell, apparently remembered where the barrel of money had sunk on the Dead River. Four years later the two simple farmers from Vassalboro purchased three large land parcels for over $4000 dollars along the Kennebec as noted on the bill of sale for "gold and silver coin to me paid in hand by John and Nehemiah Getchell of said Vassalborough."

According to Thomas Desjardin, one of their descendants, Frank Getchell, said it was family tradition that the Getchell brothers had returned to the Dead River and found the barrel of coins.

Good for them.

While Arnold was struggling up the Kennebec, Lieutenant Henry Mowat returned to Falmouth on October 18 to carry out his revenge for his ignominious retreat in May. Under orders from Vice Admiral Richard Graves to destroy the eastern seaports, Mowat's little fleet first shelled the town and then sent torch parties ashore to complete the destruction. More than 400 buildings and elven vessels were burned. General Washington called the burning of

Falmouth "an outrage exceeding in Barbarity and Cruelty every hostile Act practiced among civilized Nations."

Mowat then moved on to raid Boothbay before returning to Boston. Surprisingly Mowat did not return to the Kennebec to seek revenge against Samuel Thompson and the local Kennebec militia.

In mid October facing an imminent disaster, Arnold needed drastic action. He had too little food and supplies and too many sick and disabled men. Arnold pressed on, but the rear guard commanded by Colonel Roger Enos voted to turn back to Fort Western. Captain McCobb from Georgetown was among those who voted to retreat. Enos was faced with a lack of food and supplies, and was additionally burdened with the care of the sick and injured from the three first sections.

After first stopping in Brunswick, Enos went on to Cambridge. Washington wrote to Continental Congress President John Hancock on November 28: "Colonel Enos is arrived and under arrest. He acknowledges he had no Orders for coming away. His Trial cannot come on, until I hear from Col. Arnold."

Washington correctly concluded in a November 28 letter to Schuyler that Enos' flight would render Arnold "incapable of making a successful attack on Quebec."

Enos was later court martialed on December 1 for "quitting without leave" or more formally "leaving his commanding Officer without permission or orders." He was acquitted, based on the testimony of McCobb and the other officers then in Cambridge.

Enos later became colonel of the 16th Connecticut Regiment and a major general of the Vermont militia.

Captain McCobb and his surviving men returned home. McCobb returned to Boothbay where he married Sarah McFarland in 1784. He later commanded the First Regiment of Militia of Lincoln County.

Nevertheless, by November 4, Arnold's force was moving down the Chaudiere River where they entered a village of French and Native people at the mouth of the Famine River.

They had left the Kennebec River and paddled and carried their batteaux and canoes out of our story.

On November 8 Arnold's army of about 500 reached the St. Lawrence and could see Quebec. Somewhere between Fort Western and the St. Lawrence, half of the force had disappeared. On the thirteenth Arnold's army crossed the St.Lawrence River just below Quebec.

Almost two months passed before the unified commands of Arnold and Richard Montogomery finally assaulted Quebec on the night of December 30/31. Any element of surprise had been lost long ago. The British defenders were ready. The Americans and their French Canadian and Indian allies were soundly defeated. More than four hundred American soldiers were killed, wounded or captured including Arnold and Montgomery. At least seven Indians on the American side died during Arnold's expedition, and later hoped for recompense from Congress.

The Americans withdrew from Canada the next year. The idea of a fourteenth state was dead but not forgotten.

Military action on the Kennebec was scarce after Arnold'sExpedition, but many men from the Kennebec served in the continental army, navy and state militia units. The Massachusetts government maintained small scouting parties of men along the Kennebec, but there were no confrontations with British soldiers. The real action on the Kennebec revolved around loyalists and their patriot opponents.

After the excitement of Arnold's expedition passed up the Kennebec, the local population settled into low key violence and pressure on the loyalists to conform to the Patriot cause, remain as quiet as a church mouse, or abandoned their homes to escape to British controlled territory. If this pattern of behavior sounds similar to that imposed on the Wabanaki by the English, you would be right.

The Shiretown for Lincoln County, Pownalborough with about 150 families, was the center of Patriot and Tory violence along the Kennebec. The Anglican Priest Jacob Bailey with his mixed religious group of Anglicans, Huguenots, Catholic and Lutherans faced off against the Congregationalists led by the Cushing brothers, Charles, Sheriff and militia colonel, and William, lawyer, Justice of the Peace, and Judge of the Superior Court; and Jonathan Bowman, John Hancock's factor and son of Rev. Jonathan Bowman and Elizabeth Hancock., A lawyer, he was also clerk of the courts, register of deeds and judge of probate. Bowman, Bailey, Charles Cushing and John Adams were 1755 graduates of Harvard. Bowman remained a staunch Congregationalist but Bailey became an Anglican minister. The religious difference added to their rivalry, even though his wife Mary brought their children to Bailey's church because it was the only church in the area. Bailey accused Bowman of being a disruptive force during services.

Bowman married Mary Lowell Emerson and Mary Goodwin and had four children (Jonathan, William, Thomas and Mary). Bailey described Bowman as "Silent, concealed, and designing, with interest as his reigning passion, base and false in his friendships, and implacable in his resentments...a leader of men who generally feared but did not love him. Imperious in his bearing."

Bowman built a large house and his wife, Mary Lowell Emerson, filled it with expensive furnishings and staffed it with slaves and indentured servants. Bowman's house, built in 1762, is now open to the public.

Bowman, like the Gardiners and Cushing, hoped to build Pownalborough into a legal and commercial center based on land, lumber and salted fish. Bowman must have been very disappointed when Wiscasset became the legal and commercial center replacing the village and courthouse at Pownalborough.

Even though Bowman lived until 1804, he did not remove to Wiscasset when it became the county seat of Lincoln County.

The Cushings were the sons of John and Mary (Cotton) from Scituate. John Cushing was a judge of the Superior Court. William succeeded his father on the Massachusetts Superior Court of Judicature and in 1789 became one of the first justices of the United States Supreme Court.

Charles remained Sheriff of Lincoln County.

Charles Cushing, according to Bailey, was under the influence of Bowman and "entered warmly into Bowman's schemes." Moreover, "he was haughty, proud and imperious, with a most exalted opinion of his importance."

All the political and official leaders were Patriots, except for the Reverend Bailey and Selectman Jonathan Williamson, who soon was voted out of office. William Gardiner, son of proprietor Silvester Gardiner, was nearly tarred and feathered but was rescued by Nathaniel Berry and escaped to Topsham. Gardiner was captured there and later tried at a special court in 1777 and condemned as "inimically disposed to this & the other United States of America" and "dangerous to the Publick Peace & Safety." He was sent to Boston, but was not physically assaulted. In Boston the court threw out the charges and sent Gardiner back to his house "to enjoy the privileges of a free subject."

In the petition for his freedom, Gardiner blamed Jonathan Bowman and Charles Cushing for condemning him to the revolutionaries.

The Gardiners were great competitors of Bowman and Cushing for business, land and local power.

Although there were many threats, some confiscation of property and some legal actions against Loyalists, there was very little violence along the Kennebec. Some Loyalists, such as Bailey's father-in-law, the Reverend Weeks, actually fled from the Boston region to the Kennebec.

Bailey, who reportedly had been removed from a previous church assignment for being too familiar with young women, reported in his journal that on April 24, 1775, he was "assaulted by a number of ruffians." He was put under bond and "forbidden to pray for the king," leading Bailey to halt church services. But months later he was taken before the Committee of Safety for "not reading the Declaration of Independence, for praying for the king, and for preaching a seditious sermon."

More common were the spirited assemblies around the Liberty Pole erected in front of the Anglican Church and the subsequent cutting down of the pole by Loyalists.

There were many threats: "Let you first murder the Tories, those accursed enemies of our country. Not a devil of them shall continue to breathe another day." John Carleton of Woolwich was mobbed and threatened on several occasions, according to Bailey.

Bailey's refusal to read the Declaration of Independence in his church, touched off a mini-fire storm. Bailey was charged with sedition, but not jailed. Shunning, insults and poverty preceded his departure in 1778 for Halifax in Nova Scotia. From there he wrote letters encouraging Loyalists and urging the British authorities to recapture the Kennebec settlements.

John Jones, a "most obnoxious Tory," had his store in Hallowell trashed. He was tied up and dragged through water until he nearly drowned in the river, but he escaped with the help of James Winslow. After the war he returned to his house in Hallowell.

Jones, Ballard of Vassalborough and several others were charged with sedition and brought before a jury but were not found guilty because three Tories, John Patten, his brother and son, were on the jury. Justice North complained "we shall not be able to carry our point while we have such inflexible men on the jury."

Others like Bailey, Charles Callahan, the Gardiners, and Robert Twycross abandoned their homes and sometimes their families. Others like Samuel Goodwin and Carleton simply hunkered down and said little or nothing.

Confiscation of property by local committees of Inspection and Safety was common. In Woolwich Nathaniel Thwing led the local committee that seized the properties of David Phipps, Samuel Waterhouse and Phillip Goldwait.

In Pittston, Patriots erected a Liberty Pole in front of Abiathar Tibbetts' house where they assembled to celebrate or mourn news of the Revolution.

Along the Kennebec Nathaniel Gardiner, John Jones, John Carleton, William Gardiner and Charles Callahan among others were temporarily jailed and fined.

But there was no killing.

Judging from a list of Loyalists provided by Bailey to British General Francis McLean, commander of British forces at Castine, after his flight to Halifax in 1779, they were a small minority. Bailey listed 133 loyalists from the towns of Georgetown, Woolwich, Pownalborough and other scattered settlements.

Bailey wanted McLean to go to Kennebec with warships and a thousand soldiers to restore British rule.

He recommended that these "cruel persecutors who are vested with power by the usurpation" be removed: James Howard, Joseph North, Jonathan Bowman, Nathaniel Thwing, and Colonels Samuel McCobb and William Jones.

The British military never returned to restore order on the Kennebec, but they occasionally sent scouting parties to the Kennebec region. However, they did set up a military enclave at Castine called New Ireland.

The majority of residents were Patriots and either actively fought in the revolution or provided support on the home front. Others, like Sheriff and Selectmen Edmund Bridge, led efforts to deny support for the British by refusing to send wood to Boston when it was occupied by the British army.

Many fought in battles throughout the new American states but they were far from the Kennebec. Their activities have been ably described in many other books and articles, such as James S. Leamon's *Revolution Downeast*.

The Wabanaki tribes, now centered on the Penobscot River and eastward to the St. John and St. Croix rivers tried to play the British and Americans while maintaining their independence.

The Maliseets first asked the Massachusetts government to send them trade goods and a Catholic priest in exchange for their support. The Massachusetts government agreed, but no priest from Protestant Massachusetts was sent.

Then a contingent of Maliseets, Mi'kmaqs and other Abenakis traveled to Cambridge. There they met with Washington and offered to enlist members of their tribe. But Washington was leery of enlisting them without Congressional authorization and so sent them home with presents.

Washington wrote a letter to the Maliseets asking for their support and their prayers.

On June 3 Congress authorized Washington to enlist up to thousand Indians, but later made it clear they meant Indians who are "not livers amongst us, and were of hostile Character or doubtful Friendship."

In July 1776 when the Americans had retreated from Canada, the British were enlisting the support of the western and southern Indians, and the British were about to invade New York, Washington asked Congress for permission to help secure America's northeastern borders by forming an alliance with the tribes of Maine and Nova Scotia.

Both the British and Americans believed that alliances with the Penobscot, Passamaquoddy, Maliseet and Mi'kmaq tribes were the keys to securing control of the Eastern District.

Within a week of receiving Washington's letter, Congress authorized Washington to "call forth and engage in the service of the United States so many Indians of the St. John's, Nova Scotia and Penobscot tribes as he shall judge necessary." But told Washington he had to gain support from the Massachusetts government.

Washington promptly asked the Massachusetts government to raise five or six hundred Indians from the tribes of the Eastern District. A goal that would have been impossible even if the tribes had been willing.

Meanwhile, the Massachusetts government was already negotiating with Ambroise Saint-Aubin and other Mi'kmaq, Penobscot, Passamaquodyy and Maliseet leaders at Watertown. James Bowdoin, president of the Massachusetts Council and a major landowner along the Kennebec River, led the negotiations.

Saint-Aubin denounced "Old England" and pledged to support the "new England" in a treaty signed on July 19, 1776.

Some people argue that the Treaty of Watertown was the first foreign treaty of alliance and friendship signed by the United States, even though it was negotiated and signed by just Massachusetts.

Both sides agreed to defend the parties against all enemies. Massachusetts promised supplies at Machias and the Natives promised to send up to 600 warriors to enlist in the army. A first group of 150 would arrive in the spring of 1777, they said.

The Penobscots asked for support for the families of their warriors who had gone with Arnold and had been killed, wounded or captured. A request later honored.

Bowdoin told Washington that he would be informed of the issue of the Penobscots and that Washington should "order that what is right & just" and it would be done. Bowdoin also sent Washington a copy of the treaty and proceedings.

Agents were then sent to the tribes by the Massachusetts government to provide the required supplies at Machias and to enlist soldiers. When Thomas Fletcher and Francis Shaw reached the Indian villages, the older leaders argued that the younger men had exceeded their powers and they refused to become involved in the war. The older tribal leaders refused to sign the treaty.

As a result only seven Penobscot Natives led by Andrew Gilman arrived in Boston that October to enlist in the army, but "were fond of Returning back again to their Families." Washington recommended that they return home to await further orders.

Washington then quickly sent them to General William Heath where they could be properly supplied with blankets and other supplies.

In late November Major Shaw arrived in Boston with ten St. John's Indians from Nova Scotia. The Massachusetts Council sent them onto New York in a wagon "as they made some Objection to Travelling So far on Foot." Washington then told General Heath he was sending them to him "as they will be of no use to me here."

On December 24 while preparing to cross the Delaware, Washington wrote to the Maliseet and Passamaquoddy tribes thanking them for keeping the peace. He said he understood the poor enlistment response was because the young men "were employed in Hunting." He said the news "Made my Mind easy" and he hoped they would join the American army in the future.

He said he had ordered money to pay them. Washington then reminded them to "never lett the King's Wicked Councellors turn your Hearts against me and your Brethren of this Country."

The few Wabanaki along the Kennebec were peaceful and did not join either side. Congress appointed John Allan as superintendent for the Eastern tribes. When the British drove the Americans from the St. John River region, many fled south to Machias. A few Indigenous warriors fought on both sides of the British attack on Machias in August 1777. Leaders like Pierre Tomah tried to play both sides.

During the British occupation of Castine and the Penobscot area more than one hundred Mi'kmaq, Passamaquoddy and Maliseet men pledged allegiance to the British government.

During the American attack on the British in Penobscot Bay, Chief Orono and some Penobscots fought with the Americans.

As a reward Chief Orono and his tribe of forty families along the Penobscot were bullied by General Henry Knox representing Massachusetts in 1784 into moving forty miles from above the head tide to above the Piscataqua River for 350 blankets and 200 pounds of gunpowder, flints and shot. Chief Orono, described by Knox as "Oreono, an old man half Indian and half . french" protested: "The Almighty placed us on the land, and it is ours. Now should we not hold the lands as the Almighty gave them to us." But in the end the Watertown Treaty of 1776 was cast aside and the Penobscot tribe moved up river to land they still occupy.

To keep the Indians' friendship, the Massachusetts government continued to provide gifts and supplies through their truck houses. In 1779 they directed Colonel Josiah Brewer to reopen the truck house at Fort Halifax to provide supplies to the Wabanaki.

An appropriation for the truck house at Fort Western was made in November 1780, when £500 was appropriated at the request of Colonel Brewer for trade goods at Fort Western to maintain the "Friendship of the said Indians" by exchanging the supplies for "Furrs & Skins."

In 1781 the state appropriated another £500 for Colonial Brewer, truck master at Fort Halifax. The General Court also approved £300 to provide coats and firearms to the Chiefs, duffels to the tribes, a barrel of pork and 2 barrels of flour to "every family of an Indian soldier falling in battle."

Brewer was fired and the truck house closed in November 1782 after Brother Juniper Berthiaume, a French Franciscan missionary, accused Brewer of trading with the enemy and using goods designated for Indians for his personal use.

Ezekiel Pattee, town clerk of Winslow, had complained in September 1781 that Colonel Brewer had invited Indians to Fort Halifax but when supplies ran out Pattee had to personally house and support them.

Pattee and William Lithgow told the government in 1782 that the Indians "are greatly dissatisfied" but that "very few of the Indians visit" Fort Halifax for trade.

The truck house system for trade with the Native tribes ended with the American Revolution. The Fort Halifax truck house on the Kennebec was closed in 1782. Those at St. John, Penobscot and Machias had been earlier destroyed by the British and never returned to full operation.

As the war continued kidnappings and violence occurred from the Kennebec to Bagaduce.

In July 1780 Charles Cushing, Brigadier General and Sheriff of Lincoln County, was kidnapped from his Pownalborough house by the British and Loyalists led by the Tory John Jones. He was taken to Fort George in Castine. He was later exchanged and resigned his offices before permanently leaving the Kennebec.

After the British killed Captain Levi Soule at Broad Cove in the summer of 1780, General Peleg Wadsworth, who had already declared Martial Law making it treason for "aiding or secreting the enemy," hung a Loyalist, Jeremiah Baum, at Thomaston. Baum, who lived in the interior behind Damariscotta, was accused of treason for leading Loyalist and British soldiers for the purposes of kidnapping and pillaging. Baum was tried on August 24, 1780, and hung the next day on Limestone Hill in Thomaston.

Cushing was not alone in being kidnapped, General Peleg Wadsworth was grabbed on February 18, 1781, and imprisoned. He later escaped. That same month the British kidnapped General John Sullivan's brother, Captain Daniel Sullivan the commanding officer at Frenchman's Bay and after refusing to take an oath of office to the King he was imprisoned onboard the infamous *HMS Jersey* in New York harbor.

Minor conflicts continued between Natives and American inhabitants. For example, there is an interesting affidavit by four Indians near Fort Halifax that Father Juniper Berthiaume "did not advise the Indians to kill the Cow which they did kill."

When the Revolution ended in 1783 many of the American Loyalists had fled, leaving their American counterparts in firm control.

William Gardiner, one Kennebec Loyalist, summed up the loyalist point of view in a letter to Sylvester Gardiner on November

16, 1783: "My crime was too much Estate, and too much Power." Gardiner charged settlers as "those who had flown gaols for the most abandoned crimes" and "sett of wretches that was and are a disgrace to humane nature."

And so life on the Kennebec went on.

EPILOGUE

After the Revolution most of the conflict on the Kennebec revolved around the ownership of property. As early as October 28, 1783, the Massachusetts General Court appointed a series of committees to determine ownership from the Plymouth Company through the Kennebeck Proprietors. The committees gathered nearly endless information on land grants and purchases of land from the Natives. Many "deeds" overlapped and the committees found that various Native Sagamores had sold large tracts of land along the Kennebec. Many of these duplicated each other. Often settlers simply made their own small purchases from Natives or Englishmen. Just as otten settlers simply occupied land and fought off other claimants or even legal proprietors.

Even before the Revolution, settlers had come to the Kennebec and refused to pay the Kennebeck Proprietors. John Adams had worked for the Kennebeck Proprietors from 1769 to 1778 trying to force people to pay through the court process. For example, Adams had sought a court order on November 28, 1772 against Stephen Haselton of Pownalborough to seize £160 in property to pay for rent back to 1762.

After the war hundreds of small farmers, squatters and woodsmen battled the large proprietors along the Kennebec in person, in courts and in the legislatures. For more than twenty years many of these folks disguised and designated as "White Indians" literally fought to retain their lands by attacking the agents and the properties of the Kennebeck Proprietors.

Dozens of violent attacks on the person and properties of Kennebec Proprietors and their agents reached the courts, and we can assume many did not reach the legal system.

Sometimes, Loyalists who had fled the area or been forced off their land, returned to find their lands had been seized by the state or local governments and sold to others.

There was plenty of conflict, but that is another story.

For those who want to pursue that story, I recommend two books: Alan Taylor's *Liberty Men and Great Proprietors* and my own, *Fire and Ice: Henry and Lucy Knox and the Settling of Maine.*

J. Hector St. John Crevecieur in 1782 book, *Letters from an American Farmer,* provided a sadly, if somewhat exaggerated, poignant comment on the status of American Indians in the Dawnland after the American Revolution.

" They are gone, and every memorial of them lost; no vestiges whatever are left of those swarms which once inhabited this country. They have all disappeared either in wars which the Europeans waged against them, or else they have mouldered away, gathered in some of their ancient towns, in contempt and oblivion."

The historian James Leamon, made the argument that peace deprived the Indians of any strategic advantages. "During the war, the Penobscots, and especially the Passamaquoddy and Maliseets, had used their strategic importance to play the British and Americans against each other.

"After the war, the Indians lost their utility, and peace deprived them of their military significance. The Indians now became a tolerated nuisance, forced to accept whatever terms the victorious Americans wished to impose."

There would be no mercy from the Massachusetts government. As James Sullivan, later governor of Massachusetts, wrote in 1795: "if the Savages cannot be incorporated with the emigrants, or become civilized as a nation, it will clearly follow that they will by degrees be extirpated and finally cease to exist as a nation."

Sullivan's view, which echoed that of John Winthrop and other Puritan leaders, became the operating principle of the new state of Massachusetts and later Maine when it became a separate state. Since the Natives did not claim an exclusive use of the land, they did not own it under English/American law and culture. In spite of this view, Massachusetts and Maine for two hundred years asserted the validity of many land deeds signed by Abenaki leaders. Occupying tribal lands was a benefit to civilization, according to state leaders.

As noted before, Massachusetts shut down the truck house on the Kennebec during the war.

There were no groups of Indians on the Kennebec to remove, but those on the Penobscot were forced upstream beyond the tidal line in 1784. By treaties in 1796 and 1818, they gave up claims to nineteen townships or 400,000 acres in violation of federal law. A fact that enabled the Penobscot, Passamaquoddy and St. John tribes to obtain compensation in 1980 under the Trade and Intercourse Act of 1790.

In 1794 the Maliseet (St. John) and Passamaquoddy tribes were granted 23,000 acres along the St. Croix, but most lived on the east side of the river.

The Wabanaki had become marginalized to an extreme. Few remained on the Kennebec. Most of the Indians along the Kennebec had retreated to Canada. A small number of Wabanaki held firm on the Penobscot and St. Croix rivers, where they now remain in charge of a large reservation centered on Old Town.

There was no accurate accounting of Indians in Maine until after the Civil War. In 1800 only 347 Penobscots were listed by the state in the Eastern District. James Sullivan in an 1804 article for the Massachusetts Historical Society wrote: "There were various tribes within what is now the District of Maine but none of them exist at the present day besides the Penobscot Indians and the small tribe of about one hundred and thirty who live on the banks of the

Passamaquoddy River." The Federal Census did not count Native Amercians until 1860, and only one Indian was listed for that year in Maine. In the 1890 census, the first to list "self-supporting" Indians there were just 559 Indigenous People in Maine. In 2020 Indians were just 1.1 percent of the population of Maine. There were 758 people living on the Penobscot Reservation.

The Wabanaki Confederation was disbanded in 1862, but was reestablished in 1993.

The Kennebec, Wawenok, Sokolis and Androscoggin tribes no longer exist as separate entities, but the Wabanaki in Maine are well represented by the Houlton Band of Maliseet/ Mi'kmaq Nation, Penobscot Nation and Passamaquoddy Tribe.

The Wabanaki now settle their conflicts in courts and the legislative halls of Maine and the United States more successfully than they did on the battlefield.

ACKNOWLEDGEMENTS

Thanks to Katie Alleman and Mia Sigler, Brown Research Library, Maine Historical Society ; the staff at the Pohick and Fairfax City Branches of the Fairfax County Library for all their assistance; Michael Hill for his support and title suggestions, past and present; Susanne Balbo, Director, Whitefield Library; staff, Whitefield Historical Society; Peggy Konitsky, Midcoast Site Manager for Historic New England, for information on Jonathan Bowman and Pownalborough; Jackie Bennett, Librarian at Bristol, for her innumerable incidents of help in finding and locating research materials.

BIBLIOGRAPHY

Allen, Charles E., *History of Dresden, Maine*. Augusta: Kennebec Journal, Bertram E. Packard, 1931.

Allen, Charles E., *Some Huguenot and Other Early Settlers on the Kennebec in the Present Town of Dresden*. 1892.

Allen, William, *The History of Norridgewock: Comprising Memorials of the Aboriginal Inhabitants and Jesuit Missionaries, Hardships of the Pioneers, Biographical Notices of the Early Settlers, and Ecclesiastical Sketches*. Norridgewock: Edward J. Peet, 1849.

Baker, William Avery, *A Maritime History of Bath, Maine and the Kennebec River Region*. 2 vols. Bath, Maine: Marine Research Society, 1973.

Baxter, James P. ed., *A Documentary History of the State of Maine*. 24 vols. Portland, Maine: Maine Historical Society, 1869-1916.

Bragdon, Kathleen, *Columbia Guide to American Indians of the Northeast*. New York: Columbia University Press, 2002.

Burrage, Henry S., *The Beginnings of Colonial Maine, 1602-1658*. Portland, Maine: Marks Printing House, 1914.

Calloway, Colin G., *The Indian World of George Washington*. New York: Oxford University Press, 2018.

Calvert, Mary R., Dawn over the Kennebec. Lewiston, Maine: Twin City Printery, 1983.

Clark, Charles E., *The Eastern Frontier: The Settlement of Northern New England*. New York: Alfred Knopf, 1970.

Clark, Emma F. et al., *History of Madison, Maine*. 1962. reprint Picton Press, 2003.

Coleman, Emma L., *New England Captives Carried to Canada, Between 1677 and 1760 During the French and Indian Wars*. Reprint, The New England Historic Genealogical Society, 2012.

Dekker, Michael, *French & Indian Wars in Maine*. Charleston, S.C.: The History Press, 2015.

Desjardin, Thomas A., *Through a Howling Wilderness: Benedict Arnold's March to Quebec 1775*. New York: St. Martin's Press, 2007.

Drake, Samuel G. *Tragedies of the Wilderness. Or True and Authentic Narratives of Captives*. 1844. Reprint, Kessinger Publishing, 2010.

Eckstorm, Fannie H., "The Attack on Norridgewock: 1724," *New England Quarterly*, VII (September 1934) pp. 541-578.

Gawalt, Gerard W., *Fire and Ice: Henry and Lucy Knox and the Settling of Maine*. New Harbor, Maine: Pemaquid Press, 2022.

Gawalt, Gerard W., *Terror on the Maine Frontier: The Ordeal and Triumph of John Gyles*. New Harbor, Maine: Pemaquid Press, 2023.

Ghere, David L., "Eastern Abenaki Autonomy and French Frustrations, 1745-1760," Maine History, vol. 34 (1994): 2-21.

Gratwick, Harry, *Hidden History of Maine*. The History Press, 2010.

Grumet, Robert S., *Historic Contact: Indian People and Colonists in Today's Northeastern United States in the sixteenth through the eighteenth centuries*. Norman:

Oklahoma University Press, 1995.

Grumet, Robert S., *Northeastern Indians: 1632-1816*. Amherst: University of Massachusetts Press, 1996.

Gould, William, *Col. Arthur Noble of Georgetown. Fort Halifax. Col. William Vaughan of Matinicus and Damariscotta*. Portland: Stephen Berry, 1881.

Hanson, J.W., *History of Gardiner, Pittston and West Gardiner with a Sketch of the Kennebec Indians & New Plymouth Purchase*. Gardiner: William Palmer, 1852.

Higgins, Patricia M., *Hidden History of Midcoast Maine*. Charleston, S.C.: The History Press, 2014.

Hunt, Louise K., *In the Shadow of the Steel Cross: The Massacre of Father Sebastien Râle, S.J. and the Indian Chiefs*. Trenton, Georgia: Booklocker, 2023.

Hutchinson, Thomas, *The History of the Colony of Massachusetts Bay from the First Settlement in 1628 to 1774*. 3 vols. Cambridge: Harvard University Press, 1936.

Johnston, John, *A History of the Towns of Bristol and Bremen of the State of Maine, Including the Pemaquid Settlement*. Albany, N.Y.: Joel Munsell, 1873.

Jones, Page Helm, *Evolution of a Valley. The Androscoggin Story*. Canaan, New Hampshire: Phoenix Publishing, 1975.

Kershaw, Gordon E., *James Bowdoin. Patriot and Man of the Enlightenment*. Lanham, Maryland: University Press of America, 1991.

Kershaw, Gordon E., *The Kennebeck Proprietors: Gentlemen of Large Fortune and Judicious Men, 1754-1775*. The New Hampshire Publishing Company, 1975.

Leach, Douglas E., *The Northern Colonial Frontier, 1607-1763*. New York: Holt, Rinehart and Winston, 1966.

Leamon, James S., *Revolution Downeast. The War for American Independence in Maine*. Amherst, Massachusetts: University of Massachusetts Press, 1993.

Leger, Mary Celeste, *The Catholic Indian Missions in Maine (1611-1820)*. Washington, D.C.: Dissertation, The Catholic University of America., 1929.

Leger, Mary Celeste, *The Catholic Missions in Maine (1611-1820)*. Washington: Catholic University of America Studies in American Church History, vol. VIII, 1929. pp.75-84.

Limanni, Anthony M., "Life at Fort Richmond, District of Maine: From the Account Book of John Minot, Truckmaster, 1737-1742," *The Kennebec Pioneer*, Vol. 5 (1988).

MacFarlane, Ronald O., "The Massachusetts Bay Truck-Houses in Diplomacy with the Indians," *New England Quarterly*, vol. 11 (March 1938): pp. 48-65.

Morrison, Kenneth M., *The Embattled Northeast: The Elusive Ideal Alliance in Abenaki-Euroamerican Relations*. Berkeley: University of California Press, 1984.

North, James W., *Augusta, Maine*. Augusta, Maine: Clapp and North, 1870.

Peckham, Howard, *The Colonial Wars 1689-1762*. Chicago: University of Chicago Press, 1965.

Penhallow, Samuel, *The History of the Wars of New-England with the Eastern Indians, or a Narrative of their Continued Perfidy and Cruelty from the 10th of August 1703 to ...1726*. Boston: T. Fleet, 1726.

Pownall, Charles A., *Thomas Pownall, Governor of Massachusetts Bay*. London: Henry Stevens and Stiles, *1908*.

Roberts, Kenneth, ed., *March to Quebec: Journals of the Members of Arnold's Expedition*. New York: Doubleday, 1938.

Roberts, Kenneth, *Trending Into Maine*. Boston: Little Brown & Co., 1938.

Reed, Parker McCobb, *History of Bath and Environs, Sagadahoc County, Maine 1607-1894*. Privately Published, 1894.

Saxine, Ian, *Properties of Empire. Indians, Colonists, and Land Speculators on the New England Frontiers*. New York: NYU Press, 2019.

Smith, Nicholas, "The Wabanaki-Mohawk Conflict: A Folk History Tradition," Paper delivered at Ogdensburg, N.Y.

Taylor, Alan, *The Divided Ground. Indians, Settlers and the Northern Borderland of the American Revolution*. New York: Alfred Knopf, 2006.

Taylor, Alan, *Liberty Men and Great Proprietors: The Revolutionary Settlement on the Maine Frontier, 1760-1820*. Williamsburg, Va.: UNC Press, 1990.

Thayer, Henry O., "Loyalists of the Kennebec and one of them–John Carleton," *Sprague's Journal Of Maine History* 5 (1918): 3-24.

Thayer, Henry O., "The Indians Administration of Justice. The Sequel to the Wiscasset Tragedy," Portland, 1899. Collections and Proceedings of the Maine Historical Society, Series II. Vol X: 185-211.

Vaughan, Alden T., *New England Frontier: Puritans and Indians, 1620-1675*. Boston: Little, Brown & Company, 1965.

Wallace, Burnette B., *History of Woolwich, Maine: A Town Remembered*. Woolwich Historical Society, 1994.

Webster, Sereno, *A History of Indian Point, Georgetown, Maine*. Indian Point Association, 2021.

Wheeler, George A. and Henry W. Wheeler, *History of Brunswick, Topsham, and Harpswell, Maine*. Boston: A. Mudge & Sons,. *1878.*

Williamson, William D., *The History of the State of Maine from its first discovery, 1602 to the Separation, 1820*. 2 vols. Hallowell: Glaziers, Masters & Company, 1832.

Willison, George F., *Saints and Strangers*. Reprint. New York: Time Life, 1981.

Woodard, Colin, *The Lobster Coast. Rebels, Rusticators and the Struggle for a Forgotten Frontier*. New York: Penguin Books, 2005.

York, Mark A., *Patriot on the Kennebec. Major Reuben Colburn, Benedict Arnold and the March to Quebec, 1775*. The History Press, 2012.

INDEX

Abenaki, ix–xix, 1–4, 6, 9, 11, 12, 15, 17, 19–21, 23–25, 27–31, 35–45, 47–50, 52–57, 61, 62, 66, 67, 70, 71, 73, 74, 76, 78, 83, 87–89, 91, 92, 95, 97, 98, 101, 103–105, 107–110, 112–114, 116, 118, 119, 121–125, 127, 131–136, 140, 146, 154, 163

Acadia, 15, 18, 38–40, 45, 49, 55, 56, 102, 124

Androscoggin River, ix, xii, xv, 12, 13, 23, 25, 26, 44, 56, 59, 64, 92, 126

Androscoggin Tribe, xv, 13, 20, 45, 52, 56, 89, 91, 127, 133, 164

Arnold, Benedict, 141–149, 155

Arrowsic, 21, 27, 28, 31, 34, 38, 40, 50, 59, 60, 61, 64, 65, 67, 74, 75, 116, 122, 125, 129, 132, 145

Augusta, 11, 19, 117

Bailey, Jacob, 133, 137, 150–153

Bath, 3, 22, 74, 103, 137, 142

Becancour, 56, 57, 103, 112, 132

Biard, Father Pierre, xviii, 6–10

Bomaseen (Bomazeen), 42, 47, 52, 56, 65, 76, 78, 80, 83

Bowdoin, James, 107, 115, 116, 119, 155

Bowman, Jonathan, 115, 150, 151, 153

Bradbury, Jabez, 65, 95–97, 99, 102, 109, 114, 126–128

Bradford, William, 10, 12–17

Brewer, Josiah, 142, 157

Brunswick, 60, 88, 92, 105, 108, 109, 114, 116, 137, 148

Canada, x, xi, xv, xix, 7, 18, 26, 35, 36, 43–47, 52, 57, 65, 68, 69, 72, 73, 82, 87, 94, 95, 101, 103, 105, 106, 108–114, 118, 119, 121, 122, 124–131, 133, 135, 136, 140, 142–145, 149, 154, 163

Captives, xii, xiii, xiv, xviii, 1, 3, 4, 10, 20, 29–31, 33–37, 39, 42–44, 46–48, 50, 51, 54, 60, 73, 77, 80, 82, 90, 92, 103, 107–112, 114, 121, 123, 126, 132, 133

Church, Benjamin, 44, 45, 55

Colburn, Reuben, 143–145

Converse, James, 44, 45, 50

Cushing, Charles, 150, 151, 158

Cushing William, 150, 151

Cushnoc, 11, 13–15, 19, 52, 117, 118, 128, 133

Damariscotta, 16, 36, 104, 130, 158

Damariscove, 26, 36, 50, 74

Davis, Sylvanus, 17, 29–33, 43

Dawnland, x, xi, xiii–xx, 1–4, 7, 11, 12, 15, 16, 18–20, 22, 27, 28, 39, 40, 41, 43–45, 47, 49, 51, 54, 55, 59, 91, 92, 94, 102, 105, 110, 122, 124, 126, 128, 133, 135, 162

Denny, Samuel, 64, 74, 122

Dresden, 23, 115, 122, 133

Dreuillettes, Father Gabriel, 18– 20

Dudley, Joseph, 51–53, 55, 61, 73

Dummer, William, 75–78, 82, 86–89, 91, 92, 94, 96, 99, 100, 106, 116

Fort George, 5, 7, 60, 74, 87, 88, 93, 127, 128, 158

Fort Halifax, 115, 118, 119, 121, 122, 124, 125, 128, 157, 158

Fort Richmond, 64, 76, 78, 80, 92–95, 97, 104, 105, 107, 108, 113, 114, 116, 117, 122

Fort St. Georges, 74, 93, 95–98, 104, 105, 109, 117, 123, 125–127, 131

Fort Western, 11, 117, 118, 122, 143, 145–149, 157

Gardiner, Silvester, 115, 150–152

Gardiner, William, 151, 153, 158

Georgetown, 22, 31, 49, 60, 65, 67, 72, 129, 132, 137, 138, 145, 148, 153

Goodwin, Samuel, 108, 136, 144, 152

Gyles, John, xiv, 20, 42, 43, 48, 50, 56, 60, 61, 63–65, 74, 87–89, 91, 92, 97

Hallowell, 11, 135, 152

Hammond, Richard, 30, 31, 35

Harmon, Johnson, 68–70, 76, 78–82, 86

Heath, Joseph, 64, 68–70, 76, 78, 93, 94

Hocking, John, 13, 14

Hubbard, William, 27–30, 32–34, 36–38, 116

Indigenous People, ix, xi, xiii, xv–xvii, xix, xx, 15, 18, 25, 26, 46, 72, 91, 98, 110, 126, 135, 140, 142, 156, 164

Jesuit, x, xviii, 6, 7, 9, 11, 15, 18, 19, 47, 48, 67–71, 81, 86

Kennebec River, ix–xii, xiv–xx, 2–24, 25–31, 35–45, 47–53, 55–57, 59–66, 68, 72, 74–78, 87, 88, 91, 92, 97, 103–109, 113–118, 121, 122, 124–129, 131–134, 135–138, 141–153, 155, 156, 158, 159, 161–164

Kennebec Tribe, ix, xi, xii, xv–xviii, 3, 6, 9, 11, 13, 14, 20, 21, 23, 27–31, 35, 37–39, 41–45, 47–49, 51–53, 55–57, 61–66, 70, 72, 74, 75, 77, 78, 88, 91, 93, 110, 112, 113, 115–118, 124, 125, 127, 133, 138, 143, 164

Kennebeck Company, 105, 107, 108, 115–117, 133, 144, 161, 162

Lithgow, William, 109, 114, 117, 118, 121, 122, 127, 128, 157

Loron, 88, 89, 95, 97–101, 106

Loyalists, 136, 151–153, 158, 162

Madockawando, 36, 38, 41, 42, 45, 47, 100

Maliseets, xiv, xvi, xvii, 20, 39, 41, 43, 47, 48, 56, 60, 88, 91, 98, 119, 124, 131, 135, 154–156, 162–164

Massachusetts General Court, xix, 26, 36, 51, 59, 60, 67, 113, 115, 124, 126, 135, 139, 161

McCobb, Samuel, 145, 148, 153

Membertou, xvi, xviii

Merrymeeting Bay, xv, 13, 21–23, 25, 26, 36, 38, 44, 59, 60, 64, 72–74, 88, 92, 106, 146

Mi'kmaqs, xi, xvi–xviii, 37, 38, 41, 42, 49, 53, 102, 154

Minot, John, 88, 94, 98

Mohawks, xi, xii, xvii, 20, 23, 24, 61, 78, 82, 145

Monhegan, 1, 4, 17, 26, 36

Moulton, Jeremiah, 78, 81

Moxus, 27, 42, 44, 52, 53, 57, 98–101

Muscongus, 1, 16, 93, 102, 131

Natives, ix–xx, 1–6, 8–13, 15–18, 21–24, 25, 27–30, 35–39, 41–46, 48, 49, 51–57, 61, 62, 64–68, 76, 77, 79, 80, 87–91, 93, 94, 95, 97, 98, 100, 102–107, 109, 110, 113, 115–117, 122–127, 130–132, 135, 136, 139, 141, 143–146, 148, 155, 157, 158, 161, 163, 164

Norridgewock, 3, 11, 19, 20, 39, 42, 44, 45, 47, 48, 50, 52, 56, 57, 60, 62, 64–68, 70, 73, 75–78, 80, 82, 83, 85, 87–94, 98, 101, 103–109, 114, 116–119, 121, 131, 135, 143, 144, 146

Patriots, 136, 137, 142, 149–151, 153

Pejepscot, 12, 20, 44, 59, 60, 64, 92, 107

Pemaquid, 1, 4, 5, 8, 9, 11, 15–17, 21, 23, 25–29, 35, 36, 38, 39, 40, 42, 43, 45, 48–51, 62, 103–105, 114, 128, 142

Penobscot Tribe, ix–xi, xv, xix, 8, 9, 13, 15, 16, 18, 20, 24, 36–39, 41, 42, 45, 47–49, 52, 55–57, 61, 65, 67, 76, 79, 87–95, 98, 101–106, 109, 114, 121–124, 126–128, 131, 135, 136, 141–143, 146, 154–158, 162–164

Phips, Spencer, 109, 110, 113, 114, 122, 123

Plymouth Company, 2, 3, 11, 13–16, 19, 20, 22, 118, 128, 144, 161

Popham, 2–9, 11

Pownalborough, 115, 133, 136, 137, 144, 145, 150, 153, 158, 161

Pownall, Thomas, 127, 128, 131, 132

Purchase, Thomas, 12, 13, 19, 20, 22, 23, 25, 59

Râle, Father Sebastien, xix, 47–49, 52, 66–68, 70, 71, 77–80, 83, 86

Rawandagon, xvii, 20–24, 27

Richmond, 11, 12, 16, 17, 64, 66, 72, 74, 90–92, 94, 96, 98, 104, 110, 116, 117, 132

Sagadahoc, 3, 4, 9, 17, 21, 23, 26

Settlers, ix–xii, xiv, xvii, xix, xx, 1, 4, 5, 9, 11, 16, 20, 24, 25, 27, 28, 30, 32, 35, 36, 39–42, 44, 45, 47–50, 52–55, 57, 59–62, 66, 67, 70, 72, 74–78, 87, 88, 90–92, 100, 104–106, 108, 109, 113, 116, 122, 124–126, 129, 131, 133, 136, 159, 161

Sheepscot, 17, 20, 21, 28, 31, 36, 46, 106, 109, 122, 129, 138

Shirley, William, 95, 98–105, 111, 115, 117–119, 121, 122, 126

Shute, Samuel, 61–67, 71, 72, 74, 75

Skidwares, 3, 4, 5, 9

Sokolis, 52, 57, 164

St. François, 39, 56, 57, 87, 91, 92, 98, 105, 106, 108, 112, 121, 132, 140, 141, 143

Swan Island, 23, 65, 108–110, 113

Taconic, 11, 27, 29, 44, 45, 82, 117, 118, 122

Thompson, Samuel, 137–139, 148

Toxus, 48, 49, 66, 91, 93, 105, 106

Truck house, 5, 11, 13, 14, 16, 46, 50, 56, 60, 64, 91–95, 97, 99, 117, 157, 163

Vaudreuil, Phillippe, 52, 55, 61, 63, 66–68, 71, 82, 86

Wabanaki, x, xv, xvi, xx, 1, 3, 7, 9, 27, 30, 36, 39–41, 43, 45, 47–52, 54, 55, 57, 61–63, 65–67, 70, 74–77, 80, 88, 95, 98, 104, 105, 110, 116, 117, 122, 133, 149, 154, 156, 157, 163, 164

Waldron, Richard, 36–38

Washington, George, 119, 141–148, 154–156

Wawenock, xii, 8, 16, 39, 57, 89, 92

Westbrook, Thomas, 68, 69, 76, 77, 82, 86–88

Winslow, 29, 115, 118, 135, 157

Winslow, John, 11, 13, 15, 19, 22

Winthrop, John, xvi, xvii, 15, 18, 20, 53, 163

Wiscasset, 106, 109, 137, 145, 150

Wiwurna, 62, 63, 83

Woolwich, 23, 28, 30, 43, 125, 129, 130, 132, 137, 145, 152, 153

Made in the USA
Middletown, DE
16 May 2025